Published in 2025 by Provoco Publishing who own the publishing rights.

ISBN: 978-1-0686412-7-5

Cover Artwork - © Provoco Publishing
Cover Design – © Jane Murray at Provoco Publishing
Logo Design - © MJC at Martyn Carson Creative
Edited by Jane Murray

The Ninth Life of Norris

Dawn Treacher

Dedication

For Miles, for all your support and encouragement

Chapter One

October 2000

Norris' ninth life came as rather a shock. Instead of two legs he had four. Having previously suffered a shortage of hair, now he was covered in orange fur. It seemed only minutes earlier he had drawn his last breath, lying in his bed in a terrace off Dagenham High Street. Now, beside him sat two kittens, their heads almost as big as their bodies, their bewilderment as great as his own. If it weren't for the smell of cat pee and sour milk, Norris could have believed he was dreaming. No such luck.

The kitchenette was cluttered with the remnants of Elsie's supper, burnt baked beans in the milk pan, bread and butter on a plate and a stack of mugs harbouring what claimed to be tea. An exhausted tortoiseshell cat lounged beside the cupboard as Elsie snored in a chair, grey hairs escaping the plait that trailed over her shoulder and down her back. As his siblings guzzled from their mother's teat, Norris sighed.

Life as a cat was going to take some getting used to. Confined to a shabby bungalow and frequently assaulted by his energetic siblings, Norris took to sitting on the windowsill. It looked out over a garden in which dandelions and thistles thrived. His mother, if you could call her that, soon tired of her responsibilities, leaving Elsie to feed them, the rattle in her chest growing louder by the day. Milk, Norris could tolerate, though it reminded him of school days he would rather forget. The packets of slime labelled cat food were quite another thing, especially for a vegetarian, or at least that was what Norris had been, back in Dagenham before old age got the better of him. There his garden was filled with regimental rows of carrots and onions, where the birds knew better than to linger and weeds had no place.

Norris wondered what he had done in his previous life to deserve this. What he didn't realise was that this life was a reward for the eight that had come before it, lives in which Norris endured and at times conquered, the hurdles of human life. But even if Norris had realised this, it is doubtful he would have considered what was to come as a reward of any kind at all.

Elsie raised the kittens, haphazardly it may be argued, but with a love as tender as any mother could give her child. Norris loved the warmth of her lap as she slept in her chair, her fingers stroking his fur. He snuggled closer as her dreams turned to nightmares, so vivid they made her cry out for the husband who had never come home. Norris rubbed his head against her hand until her cries were once again smothered by sleep. For Norris, too, had seen terrors, smelt death as he held a gun, fighting in a war that robbed men, like Elsie's husband, of a future. But of course, Norris couldn't tell her.

It was the morning Elsie didn't wake that the new terror began, with the unanswered banging at the door and the faces that peered at him through the window as his siblings searched for food. When at last the door burst open, Norris didn't get a chance to say goodbye to Elsie, as he was snatched by the scruff of the neck and dropped into a cat carrier that smelt of pee and plastic. He barely saw the flash of lights from the ambulance before being bundled into the back of a van. Unlike his siblings, Norris crouched in the darkness, silent in the knowledge he would never see Elsie again.

Unloaded at the rescue centre, Norris soon saw his siblings disappear one by one. He couldn't say he was sorry; he had never liked them. If they had memories of what had come before, they never shared them. If anything, they shunned him as if he didn't belong there. Now he sat alone in a concrete cell with whitewashed walls, a litter tray in one corner and a heap of goo in a bowl. Of those people that walked past his pen, few lingered to pet him or take any interest at all. What put them off he never did understand, though it might have been the scowl that had taken root on his face. If the rescue centre offered new beginnings, Norris could not see them. All he saw was a hut and fellow prisoners who sat with him waiting out the end of the war, the terror he had once cheated now seemed his fate.

Chapter Two

It wasn't that Norris didn't want to be re-homed; it was just he didn't like the look of many of the faces that peered at him those last two weeks. As cats came and went, Norris gauged the potential futures on offer as people walked through the door to gawp at them. Whilst less discerning cats purred and preened, Norris soon learnt to withdraw to the back of his pen and display complete indifference.

Norris had soon caught on to the fact that none of the humans could understand what he was saying. All he could hear of his own voice were high pitched meows, his baritone voice now all but a memory. His fellow inmates were of course, a different matter entirely.

"No-one will want you if you ignore them."

Norris was growing tired of the opinions of Baxter, the tabby cat that faced him across the walkway. Baxter lazily licked his privates in full view of visitors, laughing at their discomfit.

"Well, I don't see you doing anything to help yourself, either," said Norris. "In case you hadn't noticed, there have been some rather dodgy looking characters looking around this weekend. Reckon I'm better off here."

"Suit yourself," said Baxter. "It's not my first time, so I'm holding out for someone older. It's kids, you see. I can't stand them."

Why am I not surprised, thought Norris.

The staff were equally baffled that such a young cat, just out of kittenhood, should linger there so long.

"He's just shy," said one, stroking Norris' head, a familiarity Norris was still very uncomfortable with.

"Maybe these will be the ones," she said, as a woman bustled through the door, dragging her young son behind her.

With a nose full of snot and mouth full of gum, the boy picked at Norris' fur through the wire. "What about this one, Mum?"

To Norris' horror the door to his pen opened and the boy grabbed at his tail. Now, Norris as a rule liked children, in moderation, but this one made him shudder. Something in the way the boy winked transported Norris back to a school playground where a wink was accompanied by a kick that bruised his shin for a week.

"Reckon this one would be fun," said the boy. "Look at his stupid face."

Before the boy had a chance to pull Norris' tail a second time, Norris lashed out, so fast and so fiercely that the boy just stood open mouthed as blood trickled down his forearm.

"Really," said his mother, pushing her son back towards the exit. "We were looking for something less savage."

Too late for that, thought Norris.

And so, the weeks passed, the only conversation from Baxter, until he too was bundled into a cat carrier by an older lady who reeked of peppermint with undertones of boiled cabbage. Two days later, Baxter's empty pen was taken over by a female Siamese who refused to speak to Norris at all, choosing instead to squeeze her eyes into tight slits that every so often watched him suspiciously.

Norris grew accustomed to the routine of a long afternoon nap, and he barely noticed the girl, her hair drawn back in a ponytail, a mottle of pimples below her hair line. She pulled the sleeves of her jumper down over her hands, her thumb now poking out of a hole in her cuff. She opened Norris' pen door and scooped him up.

Forgetting he was a cat, Norris called out, "What the hell..." which of course, came out as an angry meow.

"Look Mum," said Stella. "He's frowning."

"What about looking at the others?" said Mildred, still far from sure they could afford a cat at all. She picked at a tissue in her cardigan pocket, scrunching yesterday's supermarket receipt.

"But he looks so sad, Mum, and the lady said he's been here for weeks. You did say we could get one today."

Mildred looked at Norris, who by now had opened his eyes and was trying to free his legs from Stella's grip.

"It will need vaccinations and there's the food, of course." Mildred tucked her hair behind her ear and looked at the ginger cat. Norris stared back at Mildred's face, devoid of makeup but for the pencil lines where her eyebrows had once been.

"I know, but Gramps said it would be okay."

"I guess, but what if it scratches the furniture?"

"Mum, Dad's not here anymore. You don't have to keep looking for reasons to say no."

Norris pricked up his ears and stopped struggling. Stella placed him back on the knitted blanket that had been his bed for weeks now. He liked her voice. Well, why not? He'd had enough of this place anyway. So,

Norris padded out of his pen and rubbed himself against Stella's legs. He had seen the other cats do this with varying levels of success. It didn't feel right but what the heck, he had been a cat for so long now he may as well accept it.

"See, he wants to come home with us," said Stella.

Mildred just nodded. She was so used to not having an opinion she didn't even bother to think of one

Norris found himself half an hour later strapped into a cat carrier in the back of a rusty mini heading towards Grantchester Road. It was on the edge of the city but near enough for the front gardens to be decorated with last night's empty beer cans and discarded chips.

Chapter Three

Number Fifty-four Grantchester Road offered Norris his first taste of space to roam. His arrival had clearly been anticipated as, on stepping out of the cat carrier, he noticed two small dishes on the floor and a wicker basket complete with blanket over by the dresser. Stella had even taken the trouble to buy a stuffed mouse on a length of string but there was no way Norris was going to reward her by pouncing on it, no matter how many times she threw it at him.

"Maybe you're hungry," said Stella, spooning a jelly like substance into one of the dishes. Norris had grown to dread mealtimes, finding the only way he could eat the stuff was by imagining it was something else entirely. Seeing an open door, he sidestepped the bowl and headed into the hall.

"Just keep that cat out of your Grandad's way when he gets home," said Mildred.

Stella followed Norris into the sitting room. The high-backed chair in the bay window offered a view down the terraced street.

"Don't worry about Mum," said Stella, reaching out to stroke Norris' head. "Gramps will love you."

Dodging her hand, Norris jumped up onto the windowsill. The mini was parked outside. Traffic streamed past.

"You can go outside, only not for a while. Not until you know this place is your home," said Stella, sitting beside him.

Well, what was home for a cat, thought Norris,

though he preferred this place already to the overcrowded bungalow and his pen in the rescue centre. In many ways, this place reminded him of a house he once owned near London. It had the same bay window and mantelpiece, lined with photographs. Even the velvet curtains were similar, although his had been green, the colour his wife had insisted matched the three-piece suite. But she would never have tolerated a cat, she had been so allergic that even seeing a cat made her start to sneeze. It seemed rather ironic that now he was one. He never was suited to Irene.

Norris jumped down and walked around the room, noticing the wear on the carpet, the scratches on the small table. There was a bookcase lined with hard backed volumes, gold lettering on their spines and a small radio by the chair. If Norris wasn't mistaken, this place belonged to a man, and he couldn't help but wonder where Mildred and Stella fitted into it. Other than a home style magazine on the coffee table and a potted geranium, there seemed little to suggest two women lived here. Maybe they were only visiting, though that didn't make sense either.

It was only hours later, when Norris decided the windowsill was where he was prepared to sleep, that Gramps, as Stella called her Grandad, arrived home. Norris could hear Mildred calling out from the kitchen as the front door opened.

"Dad, supper will be ready in twenty minutes."

Stella, who had been listening to music with headphones on the sofa, jumped up and left Norris alone. Amongst the banging of cupboard doors, he couldn't hear much of what was being said, although there seemed to be no mention of him at all. Heavy footsteps passed outside the sitting room door, followed by a voice that made Norris sit up straight, ears pricked. The man's voice transported Norris back to a time when no light could break the darkness. The footsteps made their way upstairs.

Stella slumped back down on the sofa and stuffed the headphones back in her ears. Norris crawled under the chair by the window and stayed there, the smell of blood in his nose and an uneasiness that filled every vein in his cat body. Maybe this was some kind of sick joke or maybe hell itself. Either way, Norris didn't want to be here. For too long nightmares had wormed into his sleep in his last life, only now he was awake.

After several hours, Norris allowed Stella to pull him out from under the chair. He needed to pee urgently but realised too late that he had been shown a litter tray upstairs in the bathroom. Ashamed of his own cowardice, Norris hung his head as the pool of cat pee soaked into the beige carpet.

"What did I tell you," said Mildred, standing in the doorway. "Don't just stand there. You wanted a cat, now you can clear up the mess."

Stella looked at Norris. If cats could have an expression of remorse, this one did or maybe it was just an extension of that frown that had drawn Stella to Norris in the rescue centre.

"What's up with Gramps?" said Stella, rubbing the carpet with a dishcloth.

"He won't say, but he's been right tetchy this evening. Been down the social club like most Wednesdays, only he won't touch his supper and won't let me in upstairs neither."

"He'll be all right, Mum."

"Yeah, well it's taking some getting used to, having us here. You're right, it's probably nothing. He's getting cantankerous in his old age."

That night, Norris barely slept. Despite Stella's best efforts to make him settle in the basket in the kitchen, Norris crawled back under the chair and stayed there. That voice had been so very familiar, even after all these years and no matter what else Norris tried to think about all he could see was that gun pointed straight at him.

Chapter Four

Norris was woken by the sound of the front door. A few hours earlier, he had ventured, under the cover of darkness, into the kitchen and reluctantly emptied his bowl. He had settled down on the windowsill until footsteps on the stairs had woken him.

As the front door was pulled shut, Norris watched the figure of a man pull up the collar of his overcoat. What hair remained was swept over a crop of age spots that spread across the top of his head like a rash. As the man turned, Norris felt every hair on his back stand to attention. The last time Norris had seen this man he was nearly sixty years younger, but he would recognise those haunting blue eyes anywhere. The scar that framed his left eye had silvered. His face had filled out, his nose now more bulbous and veined, but for Norris it was the same man that had sat crouched in the darkness, sweat beading on his face. His eyes had pleaded with Norris then, the same eyes that now looked right through him. But all Norris could see was the gun that was pointed to own his head as a warm trickle of urine ran down his leg.

The man started to walk down the path to the gate. Norris shrank back into the shadow of the curtains, forgetting that now he was a cat and that the man could never recognise him as the ginger haired soldier, even if he did look back. Norris noted a limp in the man's step as he made his way along Grantchester Road before being swallowed by a mist that hung low in the sky.

Norris felt sorry for Stella, who still in her pyjamas, now cleared up the cat vomit from the windowsill. Maybe she'd take him back to the rescue centre, and like Baxter, he'd get another chance, but Stella just stoked his head.

"Must be strange here for you," she said.

It wasn't strange, thought Norris, it was terrifying, a living nightmare of guilt from which he could not wake up, and it was only the second day. In some ways he had got used to being reborn when he thought he had breathed his last. But only on one occasion before had he been reborn into a life that overlapped a previous one. A mixture of stupidity and naivety had seen him drown in his late teens. He could have borne it much better if he hadn't had to endure another life watching his best friend marry Shelley, the girl he had loved since school. Only then, he was a young child and could only watch helplessly as someone else lived the life he had dreamed of. For most of that life, Norris had seen his rebirth as some kind of punishment for messing up his chances. But now, Norris didn't know what to think any more.

Stella scoped him up. "Have you seen Gramps?" she asked Mildred, as her mother carried her tea into the sitting room, still wearing her floral print dressing gown, the one her husband had told her made her look like a spinster.

"I heard him leave very early. I do hope we haven't upset him. He took my leaving your father badly, but I hoped he would understand."

"I'll make breakfast," said Stella, carrying Norris into the kitchen. "I'll make extra, in case he comes back."

Norris felt more than a little guilty when he swiped a rasher of bacon from the pan as Stella and Mildred sat eating at the kitchen table. He had to eat something, vegetarian or not and he couldn't stomach the stuff that lay in his bowl. The fly could have it.

When her Grandad didn't return, Stella slipped Norris the other slice of bacon.

"You might as well finish it," she said.

Norris had taken a liking to Stella. It was a difficult age and unfortunately, he knew it well. When you were fifteen years old, you didn't really belong in either childhood or adulthood, instead you wavered somewhere between the two, but of course, you didn't realise that until years later. Dressed in her school uniform, her tie slung low over her shirt, her skirt only just grazing her knee, Stella grabbed her bag and kissed Norris goodbye.

"Be good, I'll be back at lunchtime to check on you." Her strawberry lip balm lingered in his fur as he watched her leave.

What do cats do all day, he thought, as Mildred snatched up her car keys and ushered Stella outside, leaving Norris all alone for the first time. And what if the man came back? Jimmy Morgan, Norris remembered the name, but then, how could he ever forget.

Chapter Five

Norris had counted six people, and twenty cars pass along Grantchester Road as he sat waiting. Waiting for what, he didn't know. He guessed Stella would be back at lunchtime as she said, until then he had no idea what to do. He had resigned himself to taking a nap when the front door opened. Thinking it must be Stella, Norris trotted out into the hall to greet her in the hope of something to eat. Jimmy Morgan closed the door behind him. Norris stopped in his tracks. Jimmy hung up his overcoat, tucking his gloves into each pocket and unwrapping the woollen scarf from a neck thinned by age. In profile, he was the same Jimmy Morgan, a square jaw line and pronounced forehead but the fair hair had weathered to a whiteness and what was left had receded to the point of no return. Norris made a dash for the stairs. Heavy footsteps followed as Norris scooted into the bathroom and curled up next to the litter tray trying not to heave. The footsteps disappeared into the room next door.

Unaccustomed to having such good hearing, Norris was surprised to find he could hear Jimmy talking to someone. He presumed he was on the telephone as Norris was sure there was no one else in the house. So, he listened.

"What do you mean, steal a car?" Jimmy's voice, though much older, was clearly recognisable.

"I never agreed to do that... now you listen here, driving is one thing, but not stealing..."

There was a pause. Norris wished he could hear what

the other person was saying.

"I won't, and that's the last I will say about it, do you hear me?"

Norris crept nearer to the door. Peering round, he could see Jimmy sitting at a small desk, his hand shaking as he held the receiver.

"I'll be there in twenty minutes."

As the receiver clicked back in place, Jimmy headed to the door. Norris was still outside when Jimmy stepped into the corridor.

Norris let out a cry, which of course came out as an elongated meow. Jimmy Morgan reached down and scooped Norris up, holding him under the belly.

"Well, look what we have here. Stella said she was choosing a cat. Hello, little fella."

Norris felt his whole body become rigid. Just feet away from him was the face of Jimmy Morgan, the man who had trusted Norris with his life all those years ago, not realising how much of a coward Norris really was. Part of Norris was relieved that Jimmy had got out of that building alive, the rest of him was grateful that Jimmy had no idea who he was holding.

Jimmy dropped Norris to the floor and disappeared into the bathroom. Minutes later, Norris watched him as he went downstairs, put on his coat, leaving his scarf on the hook and pulling the door closed behind him without bothering to button up his coat.

Well, like it or not, Norris had no choice but to stay here. He was, in fact, a prisoner. There was no way he was going to get out of any of the doors or windows, unless of course, someone left one open, or Stella eventually decided it was time he could go outside. So,

Norris started to explore. The room Jimmy had been sitting in seemed to be a single bedroom, with a narrow bed pushed up against one wall. A small bureau sat beside it, its flap down, forming a desk, a chair in front of it. Inside, the pigeonholes were stuffed to capacity with letters and papers. A pile of brown envelopes was stacked by the telephone. Norris jumped from the bed to the desk; using his paw he upset the pile, so the envelopes cascaded down in front of him. Norris recognised the final demand bills, many unopened and lots of them. By careful probing with his paw in the pigeonholes, Norris released a flurry of betting slips. He had liked to dabble himself in one life but never for the kind of amounts these suggested. The bureau had other drawers, but no matter how hard Norris tried, he couldn't find a way to open them. A shelf above housed a cluster of faded photographs in cheap frames. He recognised Mildred's younger self, and a toddler, who he guessed must be Stella.

Jumping down, Norris scouted around the one other bedroom at the end of the corridor. Two single beds with mis-matched duvets and pillows, were placed each side of what once must have been the master bedroom. Norris guessed Mildred and Stella now shared the room. A pile of schoolbooks lay beside one bed, along with a pair of trainers. A jumble of makeup and perfume bottles lined a small shelf by a mirror on the wall. The wardrobe door wouldn't close. Two suitcases were stacked on top. A grey hoodie sprawled on the floor.

Jumping onto the windowsill, Norris surveyed the scrub of garden, hemmed in on two sides by ugly concrete walls. At the end stood a fence upon which sat a well-fed tortoiseshell cat. Spotting Norris in the window, the cat pulled himself up on all fours, his back arched, and stared back, his tail hung low, twitching from side to side. Norris couldn't help thinking he was in a prison yard, all that was missing was barbed wire and a gun, though he doubted that cat needed any kind of weapon if he chose to attack.

Norris was relieved to hear the front door open again and Stella calling. She snatched him up from the windowsill and squeezed him. He was about to object when he saw she had been crying. Her eyes lids were puffy, her cheeks red. The letterbox in the front door rattled. A girl's voice laughed loudly through the gap, followed by a bang on the door. Stella squeezed Norris tighter and put her headphones in her ears.

Norris couldn't help but feel sorry for Jimmy Morgan. There was no sign of wedding photos, or any mention of a wife. If he wasn’t a gambler, he wasn’t far off. As for why Stella and her mother were camping out here, he could only guess. The feeling of guilt that Norris felt on seeing Jimmy Morgan's face grew deeper still. Would things have been different if Norris hadn’t been a coward, if he had actually done what he has been trained to do. He had no way of knowing back then what war would really be like or what it could do to a man. When he did, it was too late.

Chapter Six

For the next few days, Norris observed Jimmy from a distance. Norris was alone for long periods each day, so he found himself staring out of the window at Grantchester Road, the way he had watched cats do in his previous lives. But Norris was far from content with his lot, as he had imagined most cats were. Instead, he spent his time calculating how to escape. He had tried nipping past Stella's legs as she opened the front door, but all too quickly she scooped him up again.

"Not just yet you don't."

As for the back garden, well, none of them went out there at all. The tortoise shell cat patrolled the fence and clearly considered Norris a potential intruder in his territory. The chilled autumnal days meant the windows stayed firmly shut. Norris' paws stood no chance at opening them unless he miraculously grew thumbs and fingers.

On the plus side, Stella continued to sneak him food from her plate under the table and in gratitude, Norris curled up on her lap each evening as she watched the television or did her homework. Jimmy spent his evenings reading the paper and retired upstairs early. He spoke the bare minimum to Mildred, though he had taken to stroking Norris on the head, which unnerved Norris dreadfully.

It was a Monday morning when another brown envelope landed on the doormat, clearly marked as a red reminder. Mildred placed it on the table as Jimmy drained his tea. "Is everything all right, Dad?" she said, touching his arm. "If I can help, you only need to ask."

Jimmy snatched the envelope and pushed back his chair.

"I've got to go somewhere today, not sure I'll back in time for supper, so don't wait for me."

Norris listened to Jimmy climbing the stairs.

"I wish I could give your grandad more to help out, but they've cut my hours this month."

"Is everything okay, Mum?" said Stella, pushing aside her half-eaten cornflakes.

"Yes...I'm sure it will be. No need for you to be worrying. Best you go to school."

"I could walk, Mum."

"No trouble, I'm on my way to work anyway."

Norris slunk out to the hall and hid under the telephone table, hoping no one would notice him. Of course, Jimmy wasn't all right, thought Norris, that much was obvious.

Mildred tutted when she looked at her watch and hustled Stella out of the front door. Stella was busy stuffing books into her bag. Neither of them noticed Norris slip past them and nip behind a bush that grew next to the front door. They closed the door behind them and headed to the Mini, parked in its usual spot on Grantchester Road. Norris watched them drive off. He wondered if he would see Stella again. Well, he was out now, wasn't he, and if he didn't want to, he didn't have to go back. A drizzle in the air settled on his fur. He liked Stella, but living there with Jimmy had been just weird, a scary weird. Norris had decided to head off himself when the front door opened again. Jimmy, the collar of his overcoat turned up to shield his face from the wind, pulled the door closed behind him and headed towards the gate. Norris found himself following. He convinced himself he was just satisfying a curiosity before he left but, keeping as far behind Jimmy as he could, he saw the limp in Jimmy's left leg, giving him a noticeable gait. The figure in front of him pushed into the wind, his back slightly bent, his shoulders rounded displaying a decrepitude that Norris knew only too well. Gone was the confidence in stride, the ambivalence of youth. This was no longer the Jimmy Morgan that Norris had abandoned. This was an old man confronting his life head on, or what was left of it.

Grantchester Road seemed to go on forever, each red bricked terrace very much the same as the last. He followed Jimmy into Jubilee Street. They passed a newsagents and a hairdressers offering a promotion on perms. Jimmy stopped outside a small café, blue and white checked blinds at the windows, plastic chrysanthemums in re-used soft drinks bottles decorated the tables outside. Drizzle glistened on the plastic tablecloths. The door jangled as Jimmy went inside. Norris walked up to the window. He couldn't see, so checking there was no-one around, he jumped up onto a chair and peered inside. Norris was curious. What was so urgent that it had made Jimmy leave so abruptly that morning? Jimmy sat at a table away from the window where he had joined two other men, both already with coffees. One of them stood up. He wore a black raincoat, with dog hairs on the sleeves. His hands were heavily tattooed, his fingers stained with nicotine.

Norris couldn't see the other man clearly as he sat reading a newspaper, a cigarette between his fingers.

This was where Norris knew he should have walked away, and he probably would have done if the second man hadn't thrown down his newspaper and thumped the table so hard that the coffee slopped over the side of his mug. Norris saw in Jimmy's eyes, the same fear he had seen all those years ago, only this time, Norris knew he couldn't walk away. Not again.

Norris dived under the table as the door opened. Jimmy came through the door, sandwiched between the two men, a tattooed hand firmly planted on his shoulder.

"Looks like we need to go for a little drive, Jimmy. It might help you think more clearly."

The two men guided Jimmy along Jubilee Street. Norris followed, keeping close to the shop fronts, hard up against the wall. The two men stopped by a maroon hatchback parked at the end of the street. A plastic pot containing a cactus was taped to the dashboard. Norris hung back, crouching beside a litter bin that spewed takeaway wrappers out onto the pavement. He watched as Jimmy climbed into the back seat. The man with tattooed hands flicked his cigarette butt and ground it under his shoe. Norris watched the car drive away with Jimmy Morgan on the back seat, his face staring out of the passenger window.

Chapter Seven

Something didn't feel right. It was obvious to Norris that Jimmy knew those men, but it was clear that Jimmy wasn't comfortable with them. Norris had seen enough bad men in his lives to know these were not just drinking buddies. He remembered the telephone conversation. No, Jimmy was in trouble.

Jubilee Road was getting busier, and Norris was beginning to attract unwanted attention. He headed back the way he had come, past the café and into Grantchester Road. Rain pelted him as he dodged hurrying feet. Freedom had seemed a great idea, but now he wasn't so sure. He was trying to remember which house was number fifty-four, when a bicycle screeched past his head, showering him with muddy water. Startled, he darted backwards, off the kerb and into the road as a car hurtled past. Terrified, Norris tore down Grantchester Road, jumping over the wall of number fifty-four. He stood trembling on the doorstep. The overhang of the door frame offered no shelter. Rain dripped onto his head, a puddle forming around his paws. Great. So much for a plan.

Crawling under the bush as best he could, Norris shivered. He wished he had eaten his breakfast that morning, but he'd been too keen to get out. So, Norris waited. He convinced himself that if it hadn't been raining, he would have set out to find somewhere else to live. But who was he kidding. He was clueless as to what to do.

Sleep evaded him as cold seeped into his bones. It was

numbness rather than sleep that made him miss Stella's footsteps up the path but the jeers at the gate made him stick his head out of the bush.

"What are you doing here?" said Stella, scooping him up.

"Hurrying home to mum again," came the taunts.

Norris caught sight of two girls leaning over the gate as Stella wrapped his soggy body beneath her coat and opened the front door.

"Did Gramps let you out?" said Stella, rubbing Norris with a towel. "You poor thing, you're soaked." Wrapped in a blanket, Stella put Norris on the sofa. She boiled the kettle to make a Cup-a-Soup.

Norris had been bullied once. He got a black eye that lasted almost two weeks. But his mum hadn't cared that much. "Give as good as you get," she had said, laughing.

Norris crept onto Stella's lap. He didn't know what to do. He wondered if Mildred knew and if she did, whether she cared. But then, Norris had never been a great Dad, had he? Who was he to criticise. Over his lifetimes he had had sons and daughters but somehow, he had never found the time to care that much, something always got in the way. Except, of course, with Janice. She had been different or maybe Norris had been. War did that to people. But Janice had died before she had seen five years of life, and he could do nothing to save her. Norris snuggled closer to Stella. She fed him cheese from her sandwich.

"You could have picked a better day to go outside," said Stella. "I'll get Gramps to put in a cat flap in the back door, at least that way you can come back in when you want to."

Or get out, thought Norris, as he started to fall asleep. Stella kissed him goodbye and for the first time, Norris didn't mind. He was asleep before Stella closed the front door behind her. If he dreamt, Norris didn't remember. The nightmares didn't visit, so he slept the rest of the afternoon in the sitting room of Jimmy Morgan.

When Stella came home that afternoon she brought a tin of tuna. Norris licked up every flake.

"You shouldn't spoil that cat," said Mildred, piling the shopping on the worktop. "We can't afford it every day."

"He deserves it," said Stella. "Why would Gramps let him out in the rain like that?"

"Your grandad hasn't been himself these last few days. Something's troubling him. I'm worried about him."

"Where is he?" asked Stella, buttering a piece of toast.

"He didn't say. I can't think where's he's been all day. Maybe us being here is too much for him. I'll keep looking, but we just can't afford a place of our own at the moment."

Norris crawled under Stella's chair. He had a horrible feeling Jimmy was doing something stupid. Norris should know, he had been rather good at that himself.

When Jimmy still wasn't back by seven o'clock, Mildred and Stella put the cat flap in themselves. It wasn't perfect, but then Norris doubted he could have followed those instructions either.

"Not tonight," said Stella, locking the cat flap. "Tomorrow when it is light again."

So tomorrow, Norris could just walk out of there. Out of this bad dream, if that was what it was.

Jimmy appeared in the kitchen. His head glistened with rain; his overcoat heavy on his shoulders.

"Dad, you look exhausted. I'll warm up your supper."

Jimmy sagged onto a kitchen chair; his face drawn. "Don't reckon I could eat anything," he said.

"We put a cat flap in, Gramps," said Stella. "Hope that's okay."

Jimmy just nodded. Norris noticed the tremor in Jimmy's hand as he raised his mug to his lips.

"I'll be getting to bed," he said, taking his tea with him.

Norris jumped onto Stella's lap. Looking at him now, Norris wondered why he had been so scared of Jimmy Morgan. He was an old man, a damaged one for sure. Norris could only imagine what had happened to him that day after the gun shot shattered his calf.

Chapter Eight

Over the next few days, Norris took to studying Jimmy, who routinely left the house each morning, not getting back until late afternoon. Jimmy had become sullen, choosing to eat his supper in his room on a tray. When he re-emerged, Mildred fussed over him, but Jimmy said very little in return. Stella tried to encourage Norris to use the cat flap but when she pushed him out, he reversed straight back in. The tortoiseshell cat sat like a sentry on the fence waiting for Norris to pop out. Norris had no intention of giving him the pleasure of a confrontation, not yet anyway. The garden round the back seemed to offer no immediate access to Grantchester Road. From his vantage point at Stella's bedroom window, Norris could see an alleyway ran down the other side of the fence. Surely somewhere it led back to the main road. So, Norris settled into the routine of window watching in the morning, lunch with Stella and an afternoon of nosing about the empty house.

Mildred had clearly begun to establish her presence. First vases of fresh flowers appeared in the kitchen and sitting room, then a new picture on the wall and a mirror above the mantelpiece. It looked to Norris like she was planning on staying a while. Stella spent her evenings in front of the TV or listening to music. She rarely went out after school, and no-one called round for her. She didn't act like any teenager Norris had ever been a father to, but who was he kidding, he was no expert. Stella had tried to encourage Norris to sleep on the end of her bed, but Norris still favoured the chair by the window in the sitting room.

Stella had other plans for him. One afternoon she picked Norris up, opened the back door and plonked him down on the lawn. "Time to explore outside," she said, pushing him along, away from the doorway.

The grass was cold against his legs. The afternoon air felt damp on his face. Someone was having a bonfire. Acrid smoke blew across the fence. Norris planted his feet firmly on the ground as Stella tried to encourage him to explore. The twelve-foot-long patch of scrubby grass offered nothing to appeal. Norris noted the shed at one end, a crack across its window, several earthenware pots strewn beside it spewing weeds.

"Come on," said Stella. She picked Norris up and walked down the garden, pointing things out to him like he was a small child, seeing things for the first time. He wriggled until, admitting defeat, Stella dropped him back on the grass. To Norris' relief, the top of fence was unoccupied.

"Have a wander," said Stella, opening the shed door. Stella sat on a rusting deckchair, earphones in whilst Norris padded around the parameter. Little attempt had been made to make this a garden. A few bushes grew up against the fence and a line of mismatched concrete slabs pretended to be a path down the middle. Stella produced a book from her pocket and started to read, pulling her jacket up around her neck to keep out the chill that blew in the wind.

Still uncertain of his prowess, Norris crouched down surveying the fence in front of him. He launched himself, landing none too gracefully at the top. This jumping lark was going to take some practise. Norris could see the alleyway sandwiched between the small gardens on each side. A crisp packet, propelled by the wind, cartwheeled past him. From up there, Norris watched washing being collected from lines strung across gardens and a boy opening a back gate, trundling a bicycle onto the path. Norris became distracted. He didn't hear the tortoise shell cat creep along the fence until he felt his breath on his neck.

"So, you've come out, have you?" hissed Boris.

Norris spun round.

"Just so we have an understanding, this is my patch." The tortoiseshell cat faced Norris, his mottled tail flicking steadily. His eyes narrowed.

"Looks like we're going to have to share," said Norris, checking to see if Stella was still outside. Reading, Stella no longer seemed to be paying attention to Norris.

"I don't think so," said Boris. "My patch runs all along here to the main road. So, watch your step."

Several lives ago, Norris would have cowered and left. But not any longer. He moved closer to Boris. Boris laughed. "Cocky little sod, aren't you."

Norris swiped his paw so quickly it caught Boris off balance.

"Now look here," said Boris, steadying himself. Norris was about to swipe again when Stella grabbed him.

"Get off of him, you bully."

Bully, who are you calling a bully, thought Norris.

Boris turned to leave. "I won't forget that," he hissed as he leapt off the fence and disappeared along the alleyway.

"Can't have you getting into a fight on your first day out, can we," said Stella, tucking Norris under her arm and heading back indoors.

"Stella," shouted Mildred from the doorway. "Have you seen your grandad?" Norris noted a tremor in her voice.

"He hasn't come back yet," said Stella, popping Norris in the middle of the floor.

"There's someone on the phone for him. He got right annoyed when I said your grandad wasn't here."

"You could try calling back later," said Mildred, putting down the receiver.

"Who was it?

"No idea, he didn't leave a name, just rang off." Mildred squeezed the teabag in the mug until it burst. "I think he's betting again," she said, tipping the tea down the sink. "He promised me he'd stopped."

"You don't know that," said Stella, dunking a biscuit in her tea.

"Why would he be getting phone calls like that...I warned him."

Norris curled up under Stella's chair. That kind of debt collector didn't make phone calls. Norris knew that. They preferred a more personal touch.

When a couple of hours later, Jimmy came home, Norris was drinking milk from his dish. Mildred intercepted Jimmy in the hall. That's where the argument had started but it continued in the kitchen. Norris' fur prickled. He abandoned his milk and slunk under the table to listen.

"That's my business, Mildred. Keep out of it."

"But Dad..."

"No, Mildred. I may have taken you two in, but that doesn't give you the right to poke your nose in. You're just like your mother."

Jimmy threw his mug into the sink where it smashed in two. "Now leave me alone. Both of you."

Mildred ran out. Crying. Stella plucked Norris off the floor and followed. When the phone rang again ten minutes later no-one answered it.

Norris, tired of being squeezed, wriggled free and curled up on Stella's duvet. When Mildred came to bed later, her mascara had formed angry smudges on her cheeks. "I'm sorry," she said.

That night Norris stayed with Stella, listening to her sleep. In the early hours he made his way downstairs again, back to his usual seat in the window. The curtain was still open. Outside in Grantchester Road, a light shone in a car window. A man sat smoking. Norris could see the glow of the tip of his cigarette. An uneasy heaviness prevented Norris from sleeping. It was then that Norris decided it was time to follow Jimmy again.

Chapter Nine

When Jimmy came downstairs next morning, Norris was already pushing his way out of the cat flap.

"No fighting," said Stella, as the flap flipped back into place.

A heavy dew had settled on the grass. A quick sweep of the garden revealed no Boris. Norris leapt onto the fence and surveyed the alleyway. Now, if he had his bearings correct, he could head left down the alleyway and come out further down Grantchester Road. Jumping down, Norris checked behind for any sign of Boris before setting off. He could hear traffic on the road that ran parallel as he skirted past a pile of bin bags, a hole gnawed in the bottom of one exposing chicken bones and a used nappy. The alleyway cut down between two houses, a tall fence on either side of him. On reaching the main road, Norris turned left onto Grantchester Road, against the flow of commuter traffic. He headed back to number fifty-four and took up position under the bush by the front door. Norris noted that the car, that had sat outside for several hours last night with its clandestine light, was now gone.

For the next half hour, Norris regretted leaving the house so early. His empty stomach grumbled. Maybe Stella would have left him some of her breakfast in his bowl. When the front door finally opened, it was Stella and Mildred who appeared. Norris crouched as low as he could, the earth damp beneath his belly, their footsteps wafting the smell of leaf mould up his nose.

It was almost another hour before Jimmy emerged, later than usual. Norris let him reach the main road before crawling out from his hiding place.

Instead of turning right towards Jubilee Road, this morning Jimmy turned left, heading away from the town centre, his limp hampering his progress. Norris followed, keeping close to the inside of the pavement, hard up against the wall. Jimmy lumbered past a house, boarded up and decorated with graffiti, past a petrol station and down a side road. Worried Jimmy might notice him following, Norris held back, keeping the figure of Jimmy in his sights. The sound of a dog barking made Norris hesitate. Across the road from him a black Labrador strained on the leash, dragging its owner out into the road. Norris veered out of its way, running until the barking grew faint behind him but by then Jimmy had disappeared out of sight. Footsteps closed in behind Norris and he found himself scooped up off the pavement.

"What the hell..." cried Norris, his legs dangling from the clutches of a young boy.

"Put him down, Duncan, he might scratch you," said a woman, brandishing a dinosaur rucksack and lunch box.

"Can we take it home?" said the boy, stroking Norris behind the ear, wiping a bogey on his fur. "Maybe it's lost or a stray."

"It will have a home somewhere, Duncan, now come along, we don't want to be late, do we."

Norris squirmed. He scanned the street ahead and when he couldn't see Jimmy, he pushed out all his legs at once, his claws extended.

"He doesn't like me, Mummy," said Duncan, letting Norris jump free.

"Maybe you were hurting him," said the woman, taking her son's hand and propelling him along the pavement.

Norris ran, looking left then right. He reached a junction and had no idea which way Jimmy would have gone. *Hell*, thought Norris. To the right the road ran past a row of bungalows, to the left a path led to a communal green. A group of kids clustered round a set of swings, school bags draped over their shoulders, a cigarette passing between them.

On an impulse rather than anything else, Norris opted to go left. He ran past the swings unnoticed and past a row of terraces whose front doors opened straight onto the pavement. A woman in curlers opened her door to retrieve a milk bottle. She smiled at Norris. He gave her a wide berth.

Set back from the road, Norris spotted a group of garages. One of the garages was open and inside, propped up against a maroon hatchback, stood Jimmy. He was talking to the same men that had escorted him out of the café. Norris crept up close to the open doors, taking up position by the garage next door. A car sat outside, winched up on jacks, two wheels missing and the passenger door buckled. Norris edged as near as he could to the men, remaining hidden in the shadow of the wreck above him.

The man with tattooed hands was delving under the bonnet, oil stains covered his polyester trousers. The second man sat in the front seat. He tapped cigarette ash into the cactus on the dashboard, his eyes scanning a newspaper propped up against the steering wheel.

"You owe us, Jimmy, so there is no backing out now," said the man under the bonnet. "You pick up the motor where we tell you, then you drive it to the agreed location at nine-fifteen to get us." Frank slammed the bonnet shut. "Make sure you're not followed and don't go blabbing to anyone where you're going. You got that. Jimmy?"

"I don't know, Frank. I can't afford to get caught. There's Mildred now and her daughter and..."

"No-one wants to get caught, Jimmy. Do as you're told, keep stum and everything will go as planned. You understand? We need to be able to rely on you now Stewart is in hospital."

"But Frank, I'm not sure I can do it..."

"Well, Stewart can't, he can barely walk, and it's all arranged. You can do it Jimmy; I know you can. You and Mildred, you could use the cash, right? Well, it's simple, ain't it. You drive the getaway car, nothing else. Leave the rest to us."

Norris crept nearer still. Jimmy, a getaway driver? So, he wasn't just in debt then, he was up to his neck in shit, too. Norris thought of Stella and Mildred, making a new home whilst Jimmy did his best to screw it all up. Oh, how familiar that all sounded to Norris.

Frank cranked open the car door, pushing Jimmy inside. "Let's go, Ernie," he said, snatching the newspaper.

Norris slunk backwards, keeping out of sight as the car reversed out of the garage and drove away, leaving him standing in a cloud of exhaust fumes.

Chapter Ten

By the time Norris made it back to the fence at the bottom of fifty-four Grantchester Road, Boris was waiting for him. Seeing Norris approach, Boris sat up, his fur rippling along his back. Norris' tail sagged.

"Exploring, are we?" said Boris. "Try looking somewhere else."

Norris stared back at the tortoiseshell cat. "I'll go where I want," said Norris. He crouched, ready to jump.

"I don't think you heard me right," said Boris.

Norris misjudged the distance. His back legs missed the fence, and his front paws scrabbled to pull himself up.

"You're a pathetic excuse of a cat," said Boris. "Not so cocky now, are you?"

Norris had always thought cats could laugh, Boris certainly could. Ignoring the tortoiseshell, he launched himself down into the garden and headed straight for the cat flap. He had learnt that bullies soon lose interest when ignored, only Boris hated being ignored even more than he hated Norris. Boris sprinted down the garden, catching up with Norris just as he had put his head through the cat flap. Boris lunged. Norris felt a claw pierce his back. He had been in many brawls over his lifetimes. He remembered a group of boys had cornered him at school, jeering as Charlie MacLiven kicked him as he lay on the ground. Norris learnt to fight pretty quickly, and the same instinct soon kicked in, only now with a savagery that only war could teach you. Boris, overwhelmed by the ferocity of Norris' counterattack, slunk away, tufts of his fur missing and a deep claw wound in his neck.

Pushing his way through the cat flap, Norris collapsed into his basket. He had not seen the head of a tortoiseshell cat, but that of a man staring death in the face, as the knife Norris held had sunk into his chest, the blood warm on Norris' fingers, life draining away from the face no older than his own. As Norris plunged his claw into the neck of Boris, that man's face had morphed back into that of Boris the cat and Norris had shrunk away. He could still hear the knife as it clattered to the floor. Boris may be a bully, but he didn't deserve that. Norris curled into a ball, holding his paw over his eyes.

He must have slept because Stella's hand on his head woke him.

"You've been fighting again, haven't you?" she said, wiping a drop of blood from his ear. "How about a treat?"

Stella rummaged in the cupboard and retrieved a can of tuna. "Now don't tell Mum or she'll tell me I'm spoiling you."

Norris wondered where Jimmy was. For a moment he had forgotten the conversation in the garage.

"Never mind tuna, you've got to do something," hollered Norris. "You have to stop Jimmy before he does something really stupid."

But all Stella heard was a string of meows. Why couldn't she understand him, thought Norris. This was ridiculous. What was the point of him spying on Jimmy if he couldn't warn anyone? Norris didn't even sniff the tuna. He stalked across the kitchen and headed for his usual window seat. He washed his ear, the taste of blood in his mouth. The front door opened, and he could hear Jimmy talking to Stella in the kitchen. She carried two mugs through to the sitting room and prompted Jimmy to sit down.

"You're looking tired, Gramps. Drink your tea, it will warm you up. Why don't I get you something to eat, I'm heating some beans, there'll be enough for both of us."

"Thank you," said Jimmy, cradling his mug.

Norris stopped washing and looked over at Jimmy. Where had he been? Jimmy sipped his tea. Norris saw an old man, broken red veins in his cheeks and a tremor in his hand. He looked so different to the private he used to be. Unlike Frank and Ernie, who couldn't be much more than sixty, Jimmy must be mid-seventies by now. The whole idea of him being a getaway driver would have sounded preposterous if Norris hadn't heard it with his own ears.

Norris may have convinced himself that he had, in fact, imagined it if it wasn't for the car that again sat parked outside in Grantchester Road. The man, too fat for his suit, was chewing, his stubby fingers like that of a chubby toddler, tapping the steering wheel. In the light, Norris could see he was wearing a pink spotted tie. A red rash crawled up his neck that sagged like inflated beach rings under his chin. A crucifix hung below the rear-view mirror. Norris heard a fork clatter to the table. Spinning round he saw Jimmy, mouth open, a baked bean sliding out of it. He, too, had noticed the car.

"Are you okay, Gramps?" said Stella, pushing a napkin across the small table that stood in one corner of the sitting room. A table that Mildred refused to use for eating meals.

Jimmy pushed back his chair, wiped his chin and left the room.

"Look outside," shouted Norris, as loudly as he could.

"What's all that noise for?" said Stella, walking over to the window where Norris sat upright, glaring though the glass.

Norris carried on talking, anything to make Stella look at what he was looking at. He stood up, arching his back, his tail held straight out. He stared at the car and the driver, who had now opened his window and dropped a toffee wrapper on the pavement.

Stella seemed to have noticed. "Who's that?" she said.

"Who exactly, that's what I want to know," meowed Norris, louder still, his fur bristling along his back.

Stella looked around to Jimmy's empty seat at the table, his beans half eaten, congealing on the plate.

"I wonder if that's why Gramps left like that?"

"Keep wondering," meowed Norris.

The man in the car looked straight at Stella, then wound up the window and pulled out of the parking space. Norris hissed as loudly as he could muster.

Stella picked him up. "You know, I would swear you were trying to tell me something," she said. "But cats can't talk, can they?" She kissed Norris on the top of his head and set him down on the chair.

Norris heard Stella's footsteps on the stairs, followed by a knock at Jimmy's door that went unanswered.

He had never felt so frustrated. Norris needed Stella

to understand, to do something. What kind of sick joke was this life? Not only was Norris compelled to live with a man he had failed, and for which guilt would always plague him, now that same man was about to destroy his own family, and all Norris could do was watch.

Unable to draw Jimmy out of his room, Stella had gone back to school. Norris couldn't settle. He watched the road outside but there was no sign of the car again. He had just settled for a nap when the phone rang. Norris ran into the hall and up the stairs. He positioned himself outside Jimmy's door with his ear up against it.

"What were you doing outside my house?" said Jimmy. "You leave my family alone. You'll get your money."

Norris could hear Jimmy's foot tapping the floor, the strain in his voice as he spoke.

"Give me another couple of weeks, three tops, and I'll pay you back. Just keep away."

After a few seconds, Norris heard Jimmy slam down the receiver. When Jimmy came into the hall, Norris positioned himself outside the bathroom, where he sat washing. Jimmy looked pale. His skin had taken on a bleached hue that made the dark hollows under his eyes prominent. White stubble grew rough down his cheeks and around his chin. Norris was taken by surprise when Jimmy stooped down to stroke his head.

"How are you settling in?" said Jimmy, his large hands smoothing the fur on Norris' back.

Norris felt sick. He shouted, "Don't you know who I am? If you did, you wouldn't be showing me any sort of kindness."

Jimmy took Norris' meows to mean he wanted more, and he tickled him under the chin, which made Norris' stomach curdle. Jimmy disappeared into the bathroom.

Norris needed air and lots of it. He ran down the stairs, through the kitchen and darted through the cat flap. He let the damp afternoon air wash over his face and fill his nostrils. Now what, he thought. What could he do? No-one but Stella paid any attention to him, and she mistook everything he tried to tell her. The only way he was going to get Stella to do anything was to make her understand him and it didn't seem like he had a lot of time left. Shouting at her wasn't working. He would have to give her a sign, one she couldn't ignore. But how could a cat do that?

Chapter Eleven

Jimmy had been out for a couple of hours by the time Stella came home from school. Now was Norris' chance to try to show Stella something was wrong. Very wrong.

"You hungry?" said Stella, as Norris rubbed against her legs, purring as loudly as he could. But when Stella went to the cupboard, Norris let out a loud meow and ran from the room. He bounded up the stairs, his meows getting louder on each step.

When Stella didn't follow, Norris started caterwauling. "You have to listen to me, before it's too late."

Just as Norris thought he might actually lose his voice; Stella climbed the stairs.

"Are you in pain?" She crouched down to pick Norris up.

"No, you don't, just come in here," meowed Norris, dodging her hand and leading her into Jimmy's room. The flap of the bureau was down, and Norris sat on the little desk that it made. He rooted out the betting slips with his paws, scattering them over the surface. When Norris finally thought Stella was paying attention, he pointed with his head to the window and hissed, his back arched. The window overlooked Grantchester Road, and although the car that had been parked there at lunchtime was now gone, Norris hoped Stella would get the message he was trying so very hard to convey.

Stella sat at the desk, leafing through the receipts. Norris saw her smile slip and a paleness seep across her cheeks. Stella collected the slips of pink paper into a pile and then stuffed them into her pocket. Norris jumped onto the desk and rubbed against her shoulder, purring.

"You wanted me to see these, didn't you?" said Stella, stroking his head. "Why? Why would you do that? Mum was right about Gramps, wasn't she?"

Norris meowed. It was then that fate seemed to step in to help Norris, for the phone began to ring.

"Hello," said Stella. "Gramps isn't here. Can I tell him who called?"

Norris sat close, hoping to hear the caller but the voice was muffled, the telephone receiver covered by Stella's hair that had slipped out from its ponytail and hung messily around her neck.

"What do you mean?" Stella's shoulder flinched. "Wait... They hung up on me," said Stella, pulling Norris towards her, nuzzling his fur. "Why did you hiss at the man sitting in that car outside our house? Was that who rang?"

Norris purred, rubbing her shoulder, whispering, yes, yes, yes. Stella held him close.

"You really are trying to talk to me, aren't you. Mum will never believe me. So, Gramps is gambling again. Is he in trouble?"

Norris meowed softly, stroking her arm with his head. A tear traced its way down Stella's cheek and onto Norris' fur. Well, thought Norris, that is just a fragment of the trouble Jimmy is in, but at least it's a start.

Stella may have been listening to Norris, but Mildred most definitely wasn't.

"Slow down, will you," said Mildred, dropping her handbag onto the kitchen table along with her keys. She kicked off her shoes, the leather scraped bare on the toes. "Put the kettle on, will you. I can't feel my feet." Mildred rubbed her fat feet. Her ankles bulged.

"Mum, look at these if you don't believe me." Stella spread the betting slips over the table. "You were right, he's betting again. But it's more than that."

"I'm getting too old to stand at a till all day," said Mildred.

"Mum, listen, will you. A man called, he said Gramps owes him big time and if we know what's good for us, we'd make sure he paid up."

Mildred sipped her tea. "Really? Reckon that was the same guy I spoke to a few days ago. I'll talk to your grandad."

"But Mum, a man was watching us from his car at lunchtime. It was him, the man who phoned..."

"Now come on, a few betting debts are one thing. Your grandad can't resist the horses, but bookies don't sit outside your house. You've been watching too much TV."

"Maybe he owes more than that."

"What made you jump to that conclusion?"

Stella looked at Norris, who was sitting listening by the table.

"Did Grandad say something?"

"No, but I know..."

"You don't know and it's not your business. You shouldn't be looking through his things either. I'll talk to him, see how much he owes, but I don't know what I can do. I doubt he'll even listen to me. He's been very good to us, very understanding, after everything that happened with your dad. I really don't want to upset him and don't you go upsetting him, neither."

Norris heard the front door open. Mildred was trying to ram all the betting slips into her handbag when Jimmy walked into the kitchen, still wearing his coat. Stella stuffed her hands in her jeans pockets and edged away from the table. Jimmy snatched the slips from Mildred's handbag.

"Been snooping, have we, behind my back."

"Dad, maybe I can help..."

"Maybe you could just mind your own business for once. It's my problem and I'll sort it. It's nothing for you to bother about so don't you start nagging me. That's all your mother ever did and look at where it got her."

Jimmy scrunched the paper slips into his coat pocket, grabbed a beer from the door of the fridge and walked out.

"That cat shouldn't be at the table," said Mildred, pulling potatoes out of the cupboard. "It's unhygienic." She slammed the potatoes beside the sink. "You'd better get your homework done."

Norris followed Stella into the sitting room and curled up on her lap. She scooped him up off her lap. "See what you've done." She plonked Norris on the floor and pulled books out of her school bag. "Guess that's what you get if you listen to a cat."

That night at supper, Mildred pushed a charred sausage around her plate. Jimmy ate his mashed potato in between gulps from his third bottle of beer. Stella passed a sausage to Norris under the table. Despite being a vegetarian, Norris had grown to like sausage.

"Are you feeding that cat again?" said Mildred.

"Leave her be, will you," said Jimmy, patting Stella's hand. "I'm sorry about earlier. I've a lot on my mind."

"Maybe if you talked to us about it, we could help," said Stella.

Mildred pushed back her chair and began stacking plates, her potato untouched in a pool of gravy. Norris leapt up onto Stella's lap, keeping himself hidden beneath the tabletop.

"I don't need your help," said Jimmy. He drained the beer bottle and left it by the sink. "Stella, help your mother."

"What if he calls again?" said Mildred. "Then what?"

"I'll deal with it," said Jimmy. "My way."

That night, Norris curled up at the end of Stella's bed. This was going to be a lot harder than he had imagined and who knew how many days were left before Jimmy was meant to drive that getaway car.

"You really should get that cat to sleep in its basket. He's leaving hairs all over your duvet." Mildred climbed under the covers.

"How's Gramps?" said Stella, closing the book she had been reading.

"I've not seen him drink like that since my Mum left him."

"What are we going to do, Mum?"

Norris pricked up his ears.

"Let him deal with it, I guess. We're just guests here." Mildred switched off her side light and rolled over.

Is that it, thought Norris. He didn't sleep that night or the next. He had thought he was getting through to Stella, but now he wasn't at all sure. Being a cat sucked. He may as well be mute or even dead. He couldn't save Jimmy any more now than he could have done back in France, only then he hadn't even tried.

Chapter Twelve

Mildred and Jimmy avoided each other, their only contact being during mealtimes, where conversation flowed through Stella. Despite further attempts to communicate with Stella, Norris now found himself either ignored or tutted at. Norris was sure that preparations were under way for whatever 'job' Jimmy was planning, as he had taken to making furtive phone calls, his door tightly shut. Through the door, Norris struggled to hear what Jimmy was saying. Many of the conversations seemed one sided. Norris nosed around the other phone extension in the sitting room but despite his best efforts to dislodge it so he could listen in, all Norris succeeded in doing was knocking over the cut glass vase of tulips that Mildred had placed on the coffee table next to Jimmy's chair.

"Look what you've done," said Stella. She had found Norris drenched in water; his paws stuck in a maze of broken glass. She mopped up the water with a floral tea towel. "That was Mum's favourite vase," she said. "You really aren't helping yourself."

It was whilst Stella was drying his fur with a towel that Norris spotted the local newspaper lying under the coffee table. On the front page, below an article about a local celebrity's divorce, was the headline:

"Series of shop break-ins baffling police."

Stella picked shards of glass out of the carpet. Norris crawled under the coffee table to get a better look.

"... two jewellery shops had been raided in the last month. Police believe the raids are the work of a local criminal gang.... Police are asking for people to help with their enquiries..."

Norris crouched under the coffee table trying to read the small print.

"What are you doing under there?" said Stella. "You'll have that table over."

It seemed that each robbery had been meticulously planned and the perpetrators had left no clues that would help police identify them. Norris felt his skin tingle. I wonder, he thought. It's either one hell of a coincidence or Jimmy had got himself in the stolen jewellery business.

"Get off Gramp's paper, you're getting wet feet all over it," said Stella, flicking Norris with the now soggy tea towel.

Norris let out a wail, followed by a long series of expletives.

"And you can cut that out, too," said Stella, dropping the collected broken glass into the wastepaper basket.

Undeterred, Norris dragged the newspaper out from under the coffee table to where Stella could see it, then he pounced on it. He planted his paws firmly on the front page and pointed to the headline with his nose. "Look, for Christ's sake. Look at it!" Norris' meows escalated in pitch. He prodded the headline with his paw.

"What are you doing?" said Stella, snatching up the newspaper, shoving Norris onto the floor. A wet paw print now marked the headline, and the front page has a rip down one side. Stella sat back on her heels to read it.

"What are you trying to tell me? said Stella. "You are trying to tell me something, aren't you, I know you are. What is it that you want me to see?"

Norris ran over to the windowsill and with his back arched, he hissed, his head stretched forward, pointing again to where the cars parked along Grantchester Road. It was more frustrating than trying to play charades with a bunch of pensioners.

"No, not that again," said Stella. "Cats can't talk, and cats aren't intelligent, well, not really. Whatever you're doing, you're freaking me out."

Norris meowed as loudly as he could. Stella threw the newspaper on the floor.

"Just stop it, will you. If you're suggesting Gramp's a thief, you're wrong. He's not like that," said Stella. "I must be going mad; I'm talking to a cat!"

Stella stormed out of the sitting room and up the stairs.

"What's all the noise about?" called Jimmy, banging into the sitting room. He saw the sodden tea towel on the floor and what was left of his newspaper. The skin on his forehead scrunched into deep crevices as he lowered his head to read the headline. He stared straight at Norris who now sat beside the newspaper. Norris stared back. The last time they had stared so intently at each other, a gun was pointed at Norris' head and Jimmy's eyes had been staring out from behind a crack in a pile of wooden crates, just a flash of piercing blue in the shadows. Back then, those eyes had shown fear but now they seemed puzzled. Not for the first time, Norris wondered whether Jimmy recognised him, whether he saw something familiar in the cat's body that held Norris captive.

Jimmy stooped to pick up the newspaper. Rolling it carefully, he tucked it under his arm and left the room.

Norris seriously questioned his own strategy. Every hair on his feline body loathed the company of Jimmy Morgan, a loathing driven by self-guilt. Yet, what if Norris was approaching this all wrong. After all, hadn't Jimmy once been his friend, someone he enjoyed sharing a beer with. Norris had told Jimmy things he had never told anyone else. Secrets he was ashamed of. It wasn't Jimmy who had betrayed him. It was the other way round. Maybe Norris was trying to communicate with the wrong person. He liked Stella, he liked her a lot and although he thought he might be getting through to her, a little, it wasn't happening quickly enough. Norris realised he could either sit back and watch Jimmy throw away what was left of his life, knowing that Jimmy was only finishing what Norris had started, or he could befriend Jimmy in the hope of saving him. Saving him, not for Jimmy's sake, but for Stella's. Norris had managed to fail each of his daughters across eight past lives, either by neglect or indifference. For him, children had been clutter accumulated through a marriage, they simply got in the way of other things. If any of his daughters had reached out to him, he hadn't noticed but he wasn't sure he could watch Jimmy do the same to Stella whilst he, Norris, was forced to watch.

Whether by necessity or stupidity, Jimmy was a thief

or about to become one. Norris was sure about that much, at least. If Norris couldn't get Stella to see that in time, Norris would just have to do something himself but the only way he could do that would be to get Jimmy comfortable with having him around. The idea of curling up on Jimmy's lap made the bile rise in his stomach. Forcing it back down, he followed Jimmy out of the room and trailed behind him into the kitchen.

Chapter Thirteen

The next day, Norris trailed around after Jimmy, sitting beside him when he did the crossword, rubbing against his chair at mealtimes. The purr he had been perfecting for Stella's benefit was becoming easier and now he used it whenever he was near Jimmy. Norris tried to convince himself that the end justified the means and that even though sucking up to Jimmy went against all his human instincts, he carried on. He couldn't help wondering whether Jimmy had been involved in the last two jewellery raids. But surely if he had, thought Norris, the debt collector wouldn't be watching his house. If the gang needed Jimmy's help this time, Norris wondered what had happened to the last getaway driver?

Norris sat beside Jimmy, watching him read the newspaper. It had only been delivered five minutes earlier. Jimmy had grabbed it, having loitered in the hall rearranging the coats and stacking his shoes in rows. Norris edged closer, sitting on the arm of Jimmy's chair, purring loudly, and leaning over to read the story on page four.

"...More robberies feared as police make no progress..."

If Norris wasn't mistaken, Jimmy was reading the same story. Norris rubbed against Jimmy's arm.

"You're getting real friendly these days," said Jimmy, dropping the newspaper onto his lap. He stroked Norris firmly. "I can see why Stella likes you so much.

She deserves a little happiness. Life's been tough on her. I guess you miss her when she's at school."

Norris tentatively stepped onto Jimmy's lap.

"Hey...I'm not sure I'm that much of a cat person," said Jimmy, picking Norris up and placing him on the floor.

Norris couldn't help feeling relieved. The familiarity was a step too far and sitting on Jimmy lap was weird, seriously weird, but he needed Jimmy to be comfortable having him around. How else would Norris get to overhear conversations and maybe discover some much-needed clues as to what was really going on here. So, when Jimmy climbed the stairs, Norris followed. At Jimmy's bedroom door, Norris stood waiting to be allowed in.

"You want to come in, don't you?" said Jimmy, opening the door to let him in.

Norris scooted in and jumped up onto the windowsill before Jimmy could change his mind. Norris started washing, not that he had become comfortable with licking his own body. Nothing, absolutely nothing, would make him lick between his toes or his bottom. He'd seen cats do it, positively enjoy doing it, but no, there were definite limits that he would never cross. But right now, he didn't want to watch Jimmy, and he didn't want Jimmy to feel he was being watched either.

Jimmy pushed the door closed and picked up the telephone. Norris concentrated on licking the front of his paws, but his ears were pricked, listening.

"All right," said Jimmy. "I'll do it, but just the once, mind. I see the cops have no leads, so you haven't been lying to me."

Norris stopped washing and positioned himself to look like he was staring out of the window, but his ears were trained on Jimmy's voice.

"Next week...yeah, all right. The others will be busy, they won't miss me."

Which day, Norris shouted in his head. *How the hell am I going to stop him by next week?*

"And I just want cash, like you said. No stolen stuff...not here. I want nothing to do with that."

Jimmy replaced the receiver. Norris stared intently at the row of cars outside, listening to Jimmy shuffle across the room to the window behind him.

"You should be outside today," said Jimmy. "Reckon it'll stay fine."

Jimmy headed to the kitchen, Norris following closely behind, as he went straight to the fridge. He grabbed a beer.

Hang on, thought Norris. *It was only eleven in the morning.* Even on a bad day, Norris never hit the bottle until midday. Jimmy drained the bottle then tossed it into a bucket under the sink. He grabbed his coat, fumbling for his keys.

Oh no, you don't, thought Norris. *I'm coming with you.* So, when Jimmy opened the front door, Norris weaved between his legs and stepped onto the path where he lingered, pretending to sniff the lawn, a patch of grass peppered with tall thistles. He waited until Jimmy let himself out of the gate and again turned left.

Norris followed at a distance, dodging a young couple that sauntered arm in arm. Just when Norris thought he knew which way Jimmy was heading, he saw him cross the road and turn down a narrow side street.

Norris didn't have time to look. He darted across the road, the blare of a car horn ringing in his ears. He had to sprint to miss a moped with an 'L' plate that had appeared from nowhere. Running with four legs instead of two required a level of co-ordination that Norris did not have in abundance. As he reached the kerb, he nearly tripped over his own feet.

By now, Jimmy was halfway down Hawthorne Rise. Norris ran until he reached a lamppost and here, he waited. The litter bin beside him stank of stale chips. The wind blew a crumpled cola can down towards the kerb, oozing a stream of cola over Norris' front paws. Jimmy opened the gate to a pebble dashed bungalow, set back from the road. A motorcycle sat entombed in the lawn, wrapped in tarpaulin. Dandelions thrived in the flower beds, their borders long since swallowed by grass. Norris peered through the wooden gate. The olive-green front door was opened by Frank.

"Had a change of heart, have we," said Frank, his blue cotton jumper pulled down over a pair of polyester trousers on which bleach stains had turned the green to a strange shade of pink in a spatter pattern. He ushered Jimmy inside. "I thought you might. Noreen, put the kettle on, we have a visitor."

The front door slammed shut.

Norris skirted round the outside of the bungalow. He leapt up onto the wheelie bin which stood up against the wall. The windowsill inside was crammed with cactuses of all shapes and sizes. He could see Jimmy sitting on a floral Draylon covered settee, still wearing his overcoat. Frank was talking, gesticulating his intricately tattooed hands as if demonstrating a rain dance. Thanks to the double glazing, Norris couldn't hear a word he was saying. A woman entered the room, her red hair pulled back from her forehead, the years of grey still visible on her scalp. She handed Jimmy a mug and left. Norris was about to try the narrow window ledge when the front door opened again, releasing a scrawny terrier.

"Do your business, then," said Noreen, leaving the door open a fraction and disappearing back inside. Norris sat motionless as the terrier cocked his leg and watered a concrete plant pot, the stream of urine running down the path. The terrier headed back to the door then stopped, sniffing the air.

Norris leapt off the bin and made it halfway to the gate before the terrier caught up with him, its nose inches from Norris' tail.

"Come back 'ere," barked the terrier, scrabbling at the gate as Norris squeezed on his stomach through the gap at the bottom.

"Spike, get back here!" Noreen stood at the door; her feet crammed into a pair of velour slippers.

Norris glanced back behind him. He saw Jimmy's face at the window, the mug of tea still in his hand. Norris ran and he kept running until out of breath. He reached the lamppost. Norris hated terriers. He hated their constant yacking. It was just as well his last wife, Irene, had been allergic to fur or she might have got one, just to spite him. Instead, she had a tank of tropical fish installed in their sitting room and talked to them more than she talked to Norris. What Irene never realised was that he flicked his cigarette ash into the tank, adding the dregs of his coffee from his mug on the way to the kitchen. On one occasion, he squirted aftershave into the water. When two days later a little corpse was floating on the top, Norris had simply scooped it out and flushed it down the toilet before Irene had even removed her curlers.

Now what, thought Norris. He had begun to head back to Grantchester Road when a car drove past and pulled up outside the gate of Frank's bungalow. *Hang on,* thought Norris. *I recognise that car.* A middle-aged man waddled to the gate, stuffing a toffee into his mouth. The car he got out of was the same car that had been parked outside number fifty-four Grantchester Road. The man lumbered up the path, brushing crumbs from his jacket. He flicked a burger wrapper into the dandelions. Norris saw Noreen open the door, her hand firmly on the collar of Spike and with a smile, she invited the man in.

Now wait a minute, thought Norris. *Wasn't that the debt collector?* He was clearly no stranger to Frank and Noreen.

Norris waited. In the next hour, he was stroked by a group of teenage girls, fussed over by an old lady lugging a bag bulging with cauliflowers and sniffed at by an Alsatian that slobbered drool on Norris' head until his pimply owner pulled it away. Finally, Jimmy reappeared, alone, his shoulders slouched, his head watching the pavement beneath his feet. Norris hid himself behind the litter bin, letting Jimmy walk past, then Norris followed him back to Grantchester Road.

The sound of shouting made Jimmy look up. Stella pushed through the gate of number fifty-four, her face blotched and red, her hair trailing out of her ponytail.

A group of girls hung over the fence, shouting.

"Get out of here!" shouted Jimmy, raising a fist. "If I catch you again, you'll wish I hadn't."

The girls laughed. One threw a bottle over the gate. It landed, a spray of fizzy drink splashing onto the path. Another girl stuck out her tongue, raising one finger firmly into the air.

Jimmy slammed the gate shut behind him and bundled Stella indoors, leaving Norris on the doorstep with yesterday's empty milk bottle.

Chapter Fourteen

"How long have those girls been giving you hassle?" said Jimmy, pushing an open packet of custard creams across the table.

Stella didn't reply. She dipped a biscuit into her tea until it went soggy.

"Well," said Mildred. "You should have said something."

"What would be the point," said Stella.

"Don't you talk to me like that." Mildred stirred her tea. "I'll talk to the school. I won't have it."

"Oh great, they're going to love that. It would just give them more reason to laugh at me," said Stella.

Norris jumped up onto Stella's lap. At least Mildred cared, but Stella was probably right.

"Maybe stay home a few days. I'll tell school you're sick. Have a break from the place. I know it hasn't been easy moving to a new school."

"You'll only make things worse," said Jimmy. "Best leave things be, they'll get bored, you'll see."

Norris doubted it. They were unlikely to get bored unless they found a new target and who knew how long that would take.

Mildred stacked the mugs in the sink. "Did you see the thing in the paper about the robberies?"

"No," said Jimmy, getting up to leave.

"My friend's husband worked at that jeweller's that was robbed two weeks ago."

"You shouldn't listen to gossip," said Jimmy heading for the door.

"They hit him over the head," said Mildred. "He ended up in hospital with concussion. Liz said he had to have his head stitched."

The tremor in Jimmy's hand rattled the door handle. Norris watched Jimmy's skin whiten, heard his sharp intake of breath.

"Are you all right, Dad?" said Mildred, drying her hands on a tea towel and taking Jimmy's arm.

"Of course, I am. Stop fussing. You're just like your mother."

Norris watched Jimmy walk out of the room, dragging his left leg awkwardly.

"Was it something I said?" Mildred folded the tea towel. "He doesn't look well."

"He gets really tired, that's all, Mum," said Stella. "He's been out walking again today."

"Well, he shouldn't. Not at his age. He's nearly eighty. Beats me where he finds to go."

It seemed to Norris that Mildred's little nugget of information had been like a bullet to Jimmy. What Norris couldn't understand was why Jimmy had got mixed up with people like Frank and Ernie in the first place. Having left Jimmy Morgan for dead, Norris had no idea what had happened to him in the years that followed. Jimmy Morgan had been a decent young man, forced to mature well beyond his years by a war that demanded boys become men or die trying. Some of the privates had a mean streak about them, hostility to life and orders, but not Jimmy. He had embraced life in the army with a gentleness and a good-natured sense of adventure. Once, he had been a friend, a comrade. But now, only the face and the scars bore any resemblance to the man Norris had once known. The scar that must be hidden under his trouser leg, the scar beside his eye, the result of a fall from a gate. Norris feared that the real Jimmy Morgan had died in France.

That evening, Norris sat on the sofa with Stella, watching Jimmy doing the crossword. Jimmy always was good with words. It was obvious to Norris that Jimmy needed money but robbing a jewellery store? Was Jimmy really naive enough to think driving a getaway car removed him somehow from the crime, excused him from complicity? If he got caught, he would end up behind bars, at his age most likely die in prison, and where would that leave Mildred and Stella? *So, Jimmy owed money, well, big deal, so did lots of people,* thought Norris, *but they didn't turn to crime, so why Jimmy and why now?* There must be something Norris was missing. He had found out nothing of Mildred's husband or her mother for that matter. There were no pictures of Jimmy's wife. Maybe they divorced, who was Norris to judge. Irene, his last wife had left him eventually, though he hadn't been sorry. She had never accepted the death of their daughter, Janice, so young and so unfair. When life gave her no other children, she had pushed Norris away, blaming him, anyone. They grew apart. It was inevitable. He didn't miss her, only Janice.

Jimmy's head began to nod. Mildred took the paper and pen from his hand. "Three across is 'hydrogen'," she said, filling in the letters.

"Thanks," said Jimmy. "Reckon that's enough for tonight. I'll head up to bed."

"Dad, where's the rest of the paper?" Mildred

unfolded the paper; its front pages were missing.

"Dunno," said Jimmy. "I'm tired. Goodnight Mildred. Goodnight Stella."

"Best you get to bed, too," said Mildred to Stella, as she tidied Jimmy's chair and pulled the curtains. Stella went to pick up Norris. "Leave him downstairs. He needs to learn to sleep in his basket where he belongs. Stop treating him like a baby."

The light clicked off and Norris was left alone. *So, Jimmy had hidden the paper had he,* thought Norris. He popped his head into the wicker basket by Jimmy's chair, but there was no sign of the newspaper, so Norris headed into the kitchen.

The swing bin by the back door was small and plastic. Every time Norris tapped the flap with his paw, it flipped shut again, giving Norris just a brief glimpse of the newspaper, which sat inside, stuffed on top of tonight's dinner. Taking the ninja approach, Norris leapt at the bin, his paws outstretched. He succeeded in pushing the bin over. Its lid lay on the floor, the bin's contents spewed across the lino. Norris had grabbed the front page of the newspaper in his mouth when Stella walked into the kitchen.

"What are you doing!"

Norris turned to see Stella standing in the doorway in her unicorn pyjamas. Norris nudged the newspaper across the floor with his nose. The headline was smudged with tomato ketchup, a chip stuck to the bottom of the page. Stella picked it up.

"You did this, didn't you? Cats can't read. You wanted me to read this." Stella read the front page. "They are the same robberies, aren't they, and you wanted me to notice..."

"Stella, what are you doing?" Mildred had opened the kitchen, her dressing gown open, fluffy pink slippers on her feet. She grabbed the paper from Stella. "That's today's paper...the robberies I was talking about. What..."

"I was just..."

"Get that cat out of here and clear up that mess. I had my doubts about that cat. Maybe I was right."

"No, Mum, please. I really think he's trying to tell us something."

"Get to bed. Cats don't tell us anything, they're just cats and..." Mildred looked at the paper. "I'll keep this. For some reason your grandad didn't want me to read it, so I will."

Mildred left the room with the newspaper and banged the kitchen door shut behind her.

Result, thought Norris.

Chapter Fifteen

Next morning Norris could sense there had been a disagreement between Jimmy and Mildred. Mildred slammed the kitchen cupboards. Stella chose to eat her breakfast in the sitting room with the plate balanced on her knee. Egg dripped from her toasted sandwich. Norris could hear breakfast TV predicting squally showers later. Leaving the sitting room, Norris popped his head into the kitchen hoping for some breakfast himself. The crumpled front cover of yesterday's newspaper, complete with ketchup smudge, lay on the table, the creases smoothed out. Jimmy's fried egg on toast sat untouched beside it. Norris fancied an egg, but Mildred flashed him a look that could curdle milk, so he left in search of Jimmy.

Norris found him upstairs, shaving in front of the bathroom mirror, a streak of shaving foam across his chin. "Morning, puss. Guess I best keep out of the way this morning. Women! Why are they so annoying?"

Personally, Norris agreed. He had always managed to pick women that annoyed the hell out of him, but this time Mildred was right. Determined not to leave Jimmy alone, Norris ignored Stella's calls of goodbye and followed Jimmy into his bedroom. Jimmy waited to hear the latch on the front door before picking up the telephone. Norris settled himself on the windowsill. He watched Mildred and Stella climb into the Mini.

"You never told me you bashed anyone," said Jimmy. "What do you mean they deserved it?"

Norris heard a tremor in Jimmy's voice.
"I don't know that I want to do it anymore. You've not been straight with me..."
"Just hang on a minute...all right...I'll meet you in the café...twenty minutes."
Jimmy slammed down the telephone. He joined Norris at the window, looking out at Mildred's empty parking space. With some difficulty, Jimmy knelt down on the floor by the bed and rolled back the green and brown striped rug. Norris watched, trying not to look interested. Jimmy lifted a small section of the floorboard, which had clearly been cut. He delved underneath and retrieved a bundle wrapped in a faded piece of blue cloth. Jimmy put it down beside him and untied the string wrapped around it. Inside was a roll of banknotes held together with an elastic band and a gun. The fur on Norris' back bristled, his whiskers stiffened. The gun looked old and if Norris wasn't mistaken it was army issue. Jimmy put the roll of cash into his pocket, re-wrapped the gun and replaced it under the floorboard. Carefully he re-laid the rug and headed for the door.
Norris waited until Jimmy was on the landing before jumping down from the windowsill and following him. *What the...* thought Norris. *A gun? And what was Jimmy going to do with that money.* Norris could hear Jimmy in the bathroom. Not waiting for the toilet to flush, he raced down the stairs, into the kitchen and out of the cat flap. He didn't want Jimmy to see him following him and anyway he knew his way to the café. Tearing across the garden, Norris jumped up onto the fence praying that Boris wasn't sitting the other side.

Norris had always had shit luck. Boris was ensconced in the middle of the alleyway, licking his bottom. Seeing Norris, Boris abandoned his ritual and arched his back. His fur stiffened like the bristles on an overly fat toilet brush, making him look fatter than he really was.

"Just get out of the way," hissed Norris. "I'm in a hurry." He darted to go round Boris, but the other cat was too quick. Boris rammed Norris, pushing him along the alleyway.

Norris planted his feet firmly on the ground again. "Budge, I don't have time for this." Norris knew that even now, Jimmy would be heading down Grantchester Road.

"You don't catch on quickly, do you," hissed Boris. "Keep off my patch."

There was nothing for it. Time was not going to wait for Norris. Boris clearly had a death wish. After their last encounter, Norris had thought Boris would have learnt a lesson. Clearly not, he was more stupid than Norris had given him credit for. With his newly acquired Ninja style leap, Norris flew at Boris, only Boris's reactions were quicker than Norris had anticipated. A claw pierced Norris' belly as he landed on Boris's head. They rolled tightly, clinched together, their bodies merging into one giant fur ball. It was hard to differentiate one cat from the other. With a vicious thrust, Norris freed himself. Not wanting a second bout, Norris darted off down the track, leaving Boris swiping empty air, tufts of ginger fur blowing in the wind.

Norris ran, the puncture wound in his belly

throbbing. He made it out onto Grantchester Road. At first, he couldn't see Jimmy, but then he saw his head. It had been obscured by an old lady, bent into the wind, pulling a tartan shopping trolley behind her. A small dog poked its head out from under the flap. Norris ran faster, keeping close to the wall, head down, avoiding the legs and feet of a couple of teenagers who strutted along the pavement, headphones in their ears, oblivious of Norris as he weaved past them. Norris rounded the corner into Jubilee Street and saw Jimmy limp past the hairdressers. Norris was getting tired of running. A hot pain stretched across his chest. The pads of his paws ached, and a burning pain ate at the wound in his belly.

Five minutes after Jimmy had entered the Café, Norris crawled under one of the outside tables. He looked at his belly. Blood oozed from the wound. Norris licked it. The taste of fresh blood transported him back to France. Back then, his teeth had cut through his tongue, filling his mouth with blood as he dangled beneath his parachute, its strings caught in the branches of an apple tree, his legs just inches above the ground.

Remembering Jimmy, Norris jumped up onto the table, pushing his way between a bottle of plastic chrysanthemums and an ashtray. He peered inside the café window. Jimmy was sitting at a table. Beside him sat Frank, Ernie and Noreen. Noreen was eating her way through a stack of buttered toast, the froth of her cappuccino lining her top lip. The morning held an unseasonal warmth and the café's window had been pushed open. Inside Norris could hear a young waitress, proffering a glass jug, offering more coffee to an old lady who occupied a table by the window. The waitress spotted Norris and frowned.

"Count me out." Jimmy stirred his coffee.

Noreen turned to her husband, his tattooed hands hugging his mug. "Frank, just tell him, he owes me. He owes my sister."

"Noreen's right," said Frank. "You're family and that what's families do. You never minded the cash in the past."

For the first time Norris heard Ernie speak. He wore a crudely knitted jumper that dwarfed his bony frame. "If he don't want to do it, I say forget it. We can find someone else."

"Ernie, you know we don't have time to find someone else," said Frank.

Norris edged nearer to the open window. The smell of cooked bacon made his stomach rumble. He saw Jimmy nudge Frank and try to pass him something under the table. Frank's face stiffened; his lips taut.

"Put that away. It's yours, God knows you need it."

"I want out," said Jimmy.

"It's too late for that," said Frank. "There'll be plenty more where that came from. All you have to do is keep your mouth shut and do what I say."

Jimmy pushed back his chair. Whatever he said next, Norris didn't hear as a pair of hands grabbed him around his middle, lifted him up off the plastic tablecloth and dumped him onto the pavement. A foot tapped his backside.

"Scram, and don't come sniffing round here again." The waitress, her apron stained around the pocket, shooed Norris down the pavement. The door to the café opened, expelling Jimmy, his hands stuffed deep into his pockets. Norris turned to follow him.

"I said scram," said the waitress, flicking Norris with a damp dishcloth.

Forced to walk in the opposite direction to Jimmy, Norris made his way further down Jubilee Street leaving the waitress vigorously wiping the spot where he had been sitting.

So, they are Jimmy's family, thought Norris, trying to figure it out. Noreen's sister must have been Mildred's mother, Jimmy's wife. That must be the connection. Norris wondered what had happened to her and what tied Jimmy so strongly still to her family. Norris hadn't been looking where is was going. He felt breath, hot on his head. Looking up, he came face to face with a pit bull, its snout was pulled into a snarl, a drip of drool hanging from its teeth. Norris tried to shuffle backwards. The pit bull reared up, pulling at its leash, the string of drool getting longer.

"That's not worth bothering with," laughed its owner, a short man in a donkey jacket, his knuckles tattooed, his ears punctuated with an array of gold hoops. Norris backed into a pair of legs.

"Get that thing off the street," said a voice that Norris recognised.

"Mind your own business, you silly cow," said the man with a lurch, yanking the pit bull away, skirting round them before spitting into a nearby drain.

For the second time that day an arm hoisted Norris into the air, only this time it was Noreen's face that looked down at him, her cheeks smudged with rouge, the make up so thick Norris could see small cracks emerging around her lips as she spoke.

"You shouldn't be here," she said, stroking Norris' neck. "You'll get trampled."

"What are you doing with that cat?" said Frank, peering at Norris as his wife tucked the ginger cat under her arm, stroking his head gently. "Put it down, will you."

"It might be a stray," said Noreen. "It's got no collar."

"They don't need one," said Frank. "They chip them, don't they. We best get back."

Norris struggled. Noreen's hand was touching the wound on his belly, her painted nails digging into the swelling.

"What if Jimmy won't do it?" said Noreen, lowering Norris to the ground.

"He will, I'll make him if I have to. I won't let you down, Noreen."

"Well, you so often do, dear."

Noreen and Frank left Norris on the pavement and headed on down Jubilee Street. Norris, the pain growing in his belly, turned, running past the café, the waitress now seating a new customer inside and Norris carried on running, back to Grantchester Road.

Chapter Sixteen

The pain in Norris' belly had turned to a burning sensation. The puncture wound was now edged with an angry redness, the centre bulging with pus which had formed overnight. When Stella offered him some of her fried egg at breakfast, Norris didn't even sniff it.

"What are you licking?" said Stella, pushing Norris onto her lap and laying him on his back to get a closer look at his belly.

"You've been fighting again, haven't you? Now look what you've done. Mum, we have to take him to the vet."

Mildred switched on the kettle. "Vets are expensive. Maybe it can wait."

"But Mum, it's infected, just look at it and he's not eating, either."

Mildred peered at the smelly swelling that protruded through the cat's ginger fur. "It doesn't look good. He'll probably need antibiotics."

Norris had had enough of the indignity of being mauled. He squirmed fiercely and tumbled onto the kitchen floor where he trotted out of the door, heading into the sitting room.

Jimmy sat in his chair, his head in the newspaper. Norris was worried. It seemed that Jimmy was already in trouble, falling into a pit that he was steadily digging deeper, and which may collapse on top of him. *That money was payment for something,* thought Norris and if it were hidden it was unlikely to be legal and if Frank and Ernie had anything to do with it, it wasn't winnings from the horses. No, Norris was sure of it, Jimmy had crossed a line from which there may be no turning back and Norris was the only one who could stop him. But, thought Norris, why the hell should he? The stupid old fool wasn't making it easy and why should Norris even care? So, Norris left him to die back in France. He had lived with that guilt, died with it. But he couldn't help but think about Stella. What would happen to her if Jimmy got himself locked up and why did it bother him so much? Now, when Norris saw Stella, he thought of his last daughter, Janice and what could have been. He curled up on the windowsill and closed his eyes.

"We're going to have to take a trip to the vets this afternoon, Dad," said Mildred, walking into the sitting room. "They can see us at five. Looks like I won't be able to give you much this week now."

Norris opened an eye. *Vet, did she say vet?* Norris didn't like the sound of that.

"You don't need to keep giving me money, Mildred. I'm not a charity," said Jimmy.

So that afternoon, Norris found himself back in the plastic cat carrier. Looking through the metal bars, Norris watched the legs of Mildred and Stella. He felt himself being lifted up and the carrier began to sway as someone carried him to the door. Norris realised it must have been Stella as he could see the sturdy legs of Mildred leading them down the path. The passenger door of the Mini opened and Norris was pushed inside. Stella climbed in beside him.

Mildred turned the car engine for several minutes.

"The damned car won't start. Now what?"

"We could take a bus," said Stella.

"It's too late for that. Wait here."

Mildred disappeared and returned minutes later with Jimmy, who was still pulling on his overcoat as he reached the car.

"Of course it's still legal, Mildred. I'm not useless, you know. It just so happens I have taken it out a few times recently. Wait here, I won't be long."

Mildred climbed back into the Mini. Norris saw Jimmy walk past and disappear.

"Where's Gramps going?" said Stella.

"Getting his car from the garage. He'll drive us. We'll only be a few minutes late."

It was cramped inside the cat carrier. Norris was strapped into the back seat facing Stella so all he could do was wait. He needed a pee but there was no chance of that now.

At last, they were on their way. Stella had taken pity on Norris it seemed and had the carrier positioned on her lap. As the car lurched along Grantchester Road, she poked her fingers through the bars and stroked his forehead. "We're only going to the vet," she said. "They'll make you feel better."

Norris didn't share Stella's optimism.

"So where have you been driving, Dad?" said Mildred.

"Just around," said Jimmy.

"Surely you don't need this car anymore," said Mildred. "You really shouldn't still be driving at your age."

"What I do has nothing to do with you Mildred. You're growing as bossy as your mother. Good job for you I still have it."

Norris caught only glimpses of the houses as they sped past, the predicted squally rain now blurring the street outside.

Ten minutes later, Norris found himself still in the carrier only now on the floor of a waiting room that smelt of antiseptic and wet dog. Two other cat carriers faced him across the green tiled floor. In one, an obese white cat scowled at him. In the other, a pair of black kittens watched him intently, their eyes and oversized heads dwarfing their spindly little bodies. A Doberman sniffed at Norris through the bars of his carrier before being pulled away by its owner, a squat woman, a spotted headscarf tied tightly around her head. A whippet sat trembling on the knees of an old lady, a sparkly scarf wrapped around its neck.

It was hot inside the carrier and Norris didn't think he could hold on much longer. If he didn't pee soon, he thought he would burst. The vet, a stocky man with a beard of twisted copper, called his name.

"Come on, Stella," said Mildred. "Bring the carrier."

Norris was placed on an examination table and his door was unclipped. Stepping out onto the table into the cool of the room, Norris peed until a pool of urine formed around his back legs.

"I'm so sorry," said Mildred, glaring at Norris.

Stella stroked Norris tenderly. "It's not his fault, Mum. He's not used to being in the car for so long."

"What seems to be the matter?" said the vet, who had picked Norris up and was now turning him over. Pinned on his back, Norris couldn't move. A pair of large hands moved across his belly in a far too familiar move. The swelling on Norris' belly oozed yellowish pus as the vet squeezed it. "Nothing a quick shot of antibiotics won't sort out. Been fighting, has he?"

Attacked more like, though Norris, as a large needle jabbed into the back of his neck. The sting made him wince.

"It's about time you had him neutered," said the vet, rubbing the back of Norris' neck.

"Is it really necessary? said Mildred. "The adoption paperwork did mention it."

Stella protectively pulled Norris towards her.

"I would recommend you get it done as soon as possible. Bring him back next week and we'll get it sorted."

Norris backed up into his carrier, as far from the vet as he could get.

"Will it hurt him?" said Stella.

"It's a simple enough procedure," said the vet. "Nothing to worry about."

Norris couldn't believe what he was hearing. They were talking about cutting off his balls as if it were no more than removing a splinter. "Meow!" Norris cried out, just thinking about it. *Was there no end to the indignities of life,* thought Norris. Over the course of his nine lives, he had drowned, been run over, shot at, locked up and now they were going to cut his balls off. Stella scooped the ginger cat up into her arms and squeezed him tightly.

"Now keep an eye on that wound and don't forget to bring him back next week."

Back in the carrier, Norris crouched at the back feeling sorry for himself as the car drove back to fifty-four Grantchester Road. Stella tried to reach him through the bars, whispering reassurances. Norris squeezed his eyes tight trying to keep the tears at bay as he remembered the way Janice had whispered to her pet rabbit through the netting of its hutch. That had been just weeks before she died of a fever that all too quickly had smothered all life from her tiny body.

Norris didn't want any supper that night and despite Stella trying to feed him cheese under the table, Norris refused even that.

"We can get the garage to look at your car tomorrow," said Jimmy, wiping the last of the spaghetti Bolognese sauce from his plate with a piece of bread.

"I really can't afford that," said Mildred, stacking the empty plates. "You could give me and Stella a lift this week and maybe next week. I'll look into it. It would need towing; I can't move it."

Jimmy swallowed his last mouthful, cleaning a smear from his lips with the back of his hand. "I know someone who could take a look at it. It's worth a try before paying out and anyway I need my car this week."

Well, if you think so," said Mildred, passing Jimmy a piece of kitchen towel. "Who did you have in mind?"

Jimmy paused, as if thinking carefully. "Frank will take a look if I ask him."

Norris' ears pricked up at the mention of Frank.

"Frank, you mean Uncle Frank?" said Mildred.

"He knows a thing or two about cars," said Jimmy.

"You still see him?" said Mildred, carrying the plates to the sink and dropping them into the bowl. "I thought after Mum died you would have..."

"Would have what, Mildred? He lives just round the corner. I'm sure he would take a look."

"I'm just surprised you have anything to do with him, that's all," said Mildred, squirting washing up liquid under the running tap. "I didn't think you liked him much, not after..."

"I don't need you telling me who I can and can't see, Mildred. It would be better for all of us if you minded your own business."

But Norris had every intention of investigating. *There was,* thought Norris, *much more to be learnt about Frank.*

Chapter Seventeen

Half an hour later, the front door opened, and Norris heard Noreen calling. "Mildred, any chance of a cuppa, dear?"

Norris trotted into the kitchen leaving Stella in the sitting room with her homework sprawled out over the sofa. With his ears carefully trained on the conversation, Norris nibbled the grated cheese Stella had left in his bowl.

"Oh, Noreen, it's you. I'll put the kettle on. Where's Frank?" Mildred wiped her hands on a tea towel and opened the tea caddy.

"Under the bonnet of your car. Don't reckon he'll be much longer. I'll take the weight off my feet, if I may." Noreen eased her ample bottom onto a chair and stuck out her legs, her puffy feet barely contained within scuffed white pumps. "Is that your cat?" Noreen looked closely at Norris. "I saw a cat, just like that one, the other day on Jubilee Street. I'd swear it was the same one. Come to think of it, Spike was chasing one like that in our garden..."

"Ginger cats are very common," interrupted Mildred, placing a mug of insipid tea in front of Noreen. "I doubt this one would go that far."

Norris stopped eating and positioned himself next to the leg of the table, where he could take a good look at Noreen. She sat, her bottom overflowing the seat, her hair hanging in lank swathes across a face puckered by a lifetime of frowning, a crop of blackheads spreading across a fat nose. *So, this,* thought Norris, *was Mildred's aunt, the sister of Mildred's mother.* Luckily for Mildred, there was no family resemblance.

"Must be difficult for you, having to stay with Jimmy. He's not an easy man and I should know. My poor sister put up with him for years."

Mildred sucked her teeth and stirred her tea. "We get along just fine, thank you. When Mum left him, I think he struggled and now Mum's dead, well, it seems right for me to have come back."

"Yeah well, it's tough on your Stella being moved out here, a new school and all that, away from all her friends. What happened to Greg? Finally run off with one of his floozies, did he?"

Mildred spilled her tea. "I left him, if you must know. My choice, not his. Took him rather by surprise, he was expecting egg and chips. We'll manage just fine, thank you."

"It can't be easy. Money's tight, I guess. Jimmy never was one for saving."

Jimmy appeared in the doorway. Noreen slurped her tea. Norris began washing his face and ears, keeping one eye pinned on the family dynamics that were playing out in front of him.

"No luck, I'm afraid," said Jimmy, leaning up against the work surface, stirring sugar into his tea. "Looks like it's only fit for the scrap heap."

Frank walked into the kitchen, wiping his hands down the legs of his trousers that were more oil than fabric. "Got another cuppa in the pot?"

"Didn't we see a cat just like this one," said Noreen, reaching out a flabby arm towards Norris.

Norris backed up as far away as he could until his

back end was up against one of the cupboard doors.

"Best leave him alone," said Mildred, shielding Norris with her legs. "He's been to the vet today and he's not himself."

"Never took Jimmy as a cat man," said Noreen.

"I could look out for another car for you, Mildred," said Frank. "Give us a week or so. Mildred can catch the bus to the shop, can't she, Jimmy?" Frank looked at Jimmy.

Norris squirmed out from behind Mildred's legs and leapt up onto an empty chair, two seats away from Noreen.

"Dad can give me a lift this week, can't you, Dad? It would give you something to do," said Mildred.

Frank and Jimmy exchanged a look, one not missed by Noreen or Mildred.

"Don't go bothering Jimmy," said Noreen, pushing her empty mug away, a smear of pink lipstick on its rim.

"I don't see it that has anything to do with you," said Mildred, vigorously wiping the already clean work top, her bingo wings swinging in rhythm. Unlike Noreen, Mildred's curves were attractive, well distributed over a tall frame, even if some bits were beginning to travel South.

Stella appeared in the doorway, an oversized hoodie hanging over her skinny legs wrapped in electric blue leggings.

"Looks like you'll be walking to school this week," said Noreen. "All the other kids do." She reached over the table and tickled Norris under the chin with stubby fingers, the nails chewed down to the quick.

"So do I usually," said Stella. She spotted Norris and much to his relief, picked him up, clutching him protectively towards her. From Stella's arms, Norris could see the glances being exchanged between Jimmy and Mildred.

"We'll see," said Jimmy.

"Yes, well..." Noreen stood up, grabbing her husband's arm. "Reckon we're finished here, Frank. Best get back."

"I'll see you out," said Mildred, pushing past Jimmy and ushering Frank and Noreen to the front door. Norris wriggled free from Stella's arms and ran along behind Mildred into the hallway.

"Jimmy isn't suited to having a woman in the house. Best be looking for a place of your own soon, leave him be."

"What are you saying?" said Mildred, opening the front door.

"He's already shown he's not capable of looking after a woman, you're best out of here, if you know what I mean."

"Come on, Noreen." Frank pulled his wife out of the door.

"It wasn't Dad's fault that your sister was an alcoholic."

Noreen swung round, heaving one leg back onto the doorstep. "And what drove her to it, do you think?"

Mildred shut the door in Noreen's face. Norris crawled under the hall table. Stella quietly walked upstairs leaving Jimmy and Mildred in the hallway.

"There was no need for that," said Jimmy. "They were trying to help."

"Were they?" said Mildred. "Somehow I doubt that." She took off her apron, flinging it over the end of the bannisters and headed upstairs after Stella. "And I'd very much appreciate a lift tomorrow."

Chapter Eighteen

The arguing started an hour later. Norris curled up on the end of Stella's bed. Stella was reading a book, or at least appeared to be, though the pages of the utopian novel rarely turned. Norris heard Mildred walking up to Jimmy's room along the corridor. "Of course you could give me a lift tomorrow. Why have you changed your mind? It will only take you half an hour. It'll take me an hour to get to work if I have to go by bus."

"Mildred, I may have given you a home until you sort yourself out, but I'm not your personal taxi."

Norris listened through the Stella's open bedroom door.

"It's just for a few days. What do you need the car for anyway?"

"That's none of your business, Mildred."

"What about Stella? You know she's being picked on walking to school, that's why I started driving her."

Stella must have heard that, too. She stuffed a torn piece of paper between the pages and dropped the book on the floor. She tugged the duvet above her head tipping Norris further down the bed.

"She'll manage," said Jimmy. "Now, if you don't mind, I want to get to bed."

Norris heard Jimmy close his door but that didn't stop Mildred. "If you're going into town, you could just go a bit later. The betting shop opens all day."

Jimmy opened his door, his voice two octaves higher. "What I choose to do is up to me, Mildred, but for your information I'm not going to the betting office. I stopped all that, so don't go prying into stuff that doesn't concern you."

"Then what's so important about tomorrow? Can't it wait a few days? If you don't want to take me yourself, I could just borrow the car. You could walk into town, like you usually do."

"Stop it, Mildred." Jimmy shouted these last words before slamming his door shut.

Stella reached out over the duvet, pulling Norris towards her. He felt the wet of her tears on his head as she put her face against his. Norris wished he could hug her back. He regretted not hugging his own daughters more. He remembered now the rows, his incompatibility with the women he had chosen to live with, a trait that ran through all too many of his eight previous lives. He rubbed his feline head against Stella's. All except his last daughter, Janice. He loved that little girl like he had never loved anyone or anything before. He had hugged her throughout those brief years, a little miracle born after the years of darkness and fear, but all too quickly she had been snuffed out.

Mildred threw herself down on the bed beside them. "Why does he have to be so disagreeable? Surely, I'm not asking that much."

"Maybe he's busy Mum, and just doesn't want to say why."

Mildred sat on the edge of her bed. She pulled her jumper off over her head and then began unfastening her bra strap. Norris had no desire to watch her. He put his head between his paws and closed his eyes.

"Maybe he's got a new girlfriend," said Mildred, "or

he's joined some old man's club. But knowing your grandad, it involves betting, even if he does deny it. And what's he doing getting involved with Uncle Frank again? Mum never trusted Frank and hated that wife of his."

Norris meowed. He couldn't agree more but Mildred just ignored him and switched out the light.

Norris couldn't sleep. He knew what was happening tomorrow. The robbery. It must be tomorrow. Everything fitted, he thought, it all made sense. It had to be. And Norris had failed to do anything about it. Rain fell against the window, the wind soon hurling itself against the glass. Norris lay listening to the cars driving through the rainwater that must by now be running along the road and pavements as the rain became torrential. A crackle of thunder made Norris jump. Tomorrow, all Norris could think about was tomorrow. *What the hell could he do?*

Next morning, Norris was woken by Stella's alarm clock. He had briefly slept, his dream vividly unpleasant. Raising his head from the duvet, Norris could hear the rain still pelting the window. He jumped onto the windowsill as Stella dressed. Mildred had already gone downstairs; he could hear cupboards banging in the kitchen below them. Outside, the sky was a deep purple, heavy with raindrops that fell thickly and relentlessly.

Stella grabbed her purple vinyl school bag and tossed in a couple of exercise books. Unzipped, she slung the bag over her shoulder and went downstairs. Norris followed her into the kitchen. Despite a gnawing emptiness in his stomach, he felt sick.

Jimmy was finishing a bowl of wheat flakes. He was dressed in an old blue jumper, suede patches at the elbows and corduroy trousers worn thin on the knees. Norris noted the tremor in Jimmy's hand as he held the spoon to his mouth. Droplets of sweat glistened on his forehead. Silver stubble had grown into a fuzziness overnight on his chin. Mildred tipped the last of her tea down the sink as thunder rumbled in the distance. "I didn't get a wink of sleep," said Mildred. She rinsed out the milk bottle before standing it on the side of the sink. "Look at it out there. I'll be drowned before I even get to the bus stop."

Jimmy's spoon rattled in the bowl as he pushed it across the table. The lights flickered. An angry streak of lightening lit up the purple sky outside the kitchen window.

"Stella, make sure you wear your raincoat, the one with the hood. No brolly is going to stay up in this for long. Don't know why I bothered doing my hair at all today."

Jimmy looked at his watch. Then he looked at Mildred. "If you don't mind being a bit early, I could take you both now."

Mildred stopped washing up. "Really?" Her voice lightened. She wiped her hands on a tea towel. "That would be great." She bent down and kissed Jimmy's stubbly cheek. "You really ought to have shaved if you are going out somewhere. And your jacket would look much nicer than that old jumper."

"Stop fussing and get your coat, Mildred. We need to

get a move on."

"Stella, coat, bag, now please. We don't want to keep Grandad waiting, do we?"

Norris panicked. Now. Jimmy was leaving now.

Stella pulled on her blue raincoat. "I've forgotten my locker key." She dropped her school bag in the hall and bounded up the stairs.

"Oh, do hurry," called Mildred.

Norris couldn't let Jimmy leave without him. Not today. Norris could hear Mildred still fussing over Jimmy in the kitchen. With no time to doubt his decision, Norris jumped into Stella's open school bag and burrowed beneath her sports kit into the end of the duffle bag. *What if Stella closed the zip,* thought Norris. Hell, he would just have to chance it. He heard more feet heading upstairs. He curled himself up into a tight ball between a hairbrush and an apple. A pair of used sports socks now covered his head muffling the voices in the hall. He heard the front door open, felt a rush of cold air. Water dripped from the guttering onto the doorstep as Jimmy shouted for Stella to hurry.

With a jolt, Stella lifted the bag and Norris found himself being carried down the path in the rain with the zip still open. The bag bounced against Stella's side. Norris didn't dare peer out as rain pelted the top of the bag and found its way through the open zip and through the layer of clothing to his head.

"Get in, you two," said Jimmy. The bag, with Norris inside, was dumped onto the back seat of Jimmy's car.

As Stella turned to find her seat belt, Norris shot out of the bag and into the foot well, crawling under the front passenger seat. Mildred wriggled into the seat above him, dropping her handbag down by her feet. The door slammed shut and the car began to move.

Hidden, Norris' heart raced. The smell of Mildred's wet shoes filled his nostrils as he felt himself moving along the road, unable to see where he was going. The wheels bumped over a pothole; the road noise close to his head. He squeezed his eyes shut and found himself back inside that pick-up truck, hidden under a sack with the young Jimmy. The truck had bounced along the rutted farm track. He could hear Jimmy's breathing, could almost smell his fear. Now, it was an old Jimmy driving and Norris felt so sick he thought he was going to puke over Mildred's bag. Part of him couldn't stop thinking, the same thought that had plagued him all those years ago, that this was a very bad idea. A very bad idea indeed.

Chapter Nineteen

The car came to a stop and Stella opened the passenger door letting in a howl of rain.

"Have a good day," said Mildred.

"Thanks for the lift, Gramps," said Stella, slamming the door shut.

Norris lay curled up underneath Mildred's seat, the movement of the car once again vibrating under his belly. The car lurched around the corner, the gear box screeching.

"Is everything all right, Dad?" said Mildred, pulling a scarf over her head and draping the ends around her shoulders. "You seem a little jumpy."

Jimmy accelerated, jolting Norris who slid out from under the seat and banged up against the back seat.

"Steady on, Dad. We've plenty of time," said Mildred, grabbing the edge of her seat.

He's late, thought Norris.

"No need to tell me how to drive, Mildred," said Jimmy, as he swung the car round to the right. "I had enough of your mother doing that."

Norris crawled back under Mildred's seat and tucked his head between his paws. He was feeling decidedly nauseous. What the hell did he think he was doing? As the car sped forwards, Norris felt himself sliding towards Mildred's ankles. He clung onto Mildred's bag to steady himself, digging his claws into the soft leather. The car jolted to a stop.

"Here you are, Mildred." The car had stopped outside a small convenience store, bunches of battered flowers heaped in black buckets outside, the wind pushing customers through the doors. "Call if you need me to collect you tonight."

Mildred grabbed her bag out from by her feet and cranked open the door. "Thanks, Dad. See you later. Take it easy, okay."

With a squeal of tyres on wet tarmac, they were off again. Norris wanted to see where they were going so he crawled up between the seats, snagging the upholstery with his claws. He pulled himself up onto the back seat, stood on his hind legs and peered out of the window. The glass was streaked with rain. Outside, the pavements were a blur of water droplets and lights rushing past too quickly for Norris to see where they were going, not that it would have helped as he had no idea where they were. Jimmy was driving too fast, too fast for the driving conditions. Row after row of houses zipped past punctuated with the bright lights of shops. People with wind battered umbrellas surged along the pavements, rain lashing them sideways. Up ahead, Norris could see the traffic grinding to a halt, the glow of a red light. Roadworks lined the pavement, their barriers streaks of orange through the rain smeared car window.

Jimmy braked. "Shit!"

The seconds ticked past. *What if Jimmy turned round now,* thought Norris. Norris shrank down onto the back seat as low as he could, his ears angled, listening. Jimmy was oblivious of the ginger cat sitting in the back of his car. Norris could hear him breathing, heavy and rough. At last, the lights changed to green. Jimmy gripped the steering wheel tightly, pulling away, his foot to the floor. He swung the car down a narrow road lined with sandwich bars and kebab shops, each bump making Norris jumpier than the last. One final turn and Jimmy pulled into a small side street.

Norris heard Jimmy kill the ignition and open the driver's door. A cold wind whipped at Norris' fur. As soon as Jimmy was out of the car, Norris leapt down from the back seat and crawled under the driver's seat, stopping next to the open door. Through it he could see Jimmy standing by a green estate car, he was inserting a key in the door lock.

The getaway car. This must be it. The switch. *Now what,* thought Norris. The key still swung in the ignition above Norris' head. He watched Jimmy open the back passenger door of the estate car, then he headed back to the boot of his own car. Not pausing to think, Norris tore out of the foot well, out across the rain drenched pavement and into the getaway car. He positioned himself on the back seat, looking out towards Jimmy. He watched Jimmy lifting a barrel bag out of the boot of his car and he was about to swing it onto the back seat of the getaway car when he spotted the ginger cat sitting on the back seat. Jimmy froze. A twitch above his left eyebrow was the only movement. The same nervous twitch that Norris had watched in the back of that truck in France, when both were young privates, hiding under sacks as they were driven across farmland in occupied France.

Norris stared back. What else could he do, thought Norris, he was a cat. Jimmy looked at his watch then at Norris, then back at his watch again. Norris wondered what he must be thinking, whether any part of Jimmy recognised him. But why should he? Norris was a cat, a rather pathetic looking one at that, with his wet fur sticking up around his neck.

At last, Jimmy seemed to click back into action. “What are you doing here, you stupid cat.” He dumped the barrel bag beyond Norris on the seat and rubbed the top of Norris’ head. “How on earth did you get here?”

Me, stupid, thought Norris. *I'm not the one picking up a getaway car for a couple of thugs when you should be sitting in your armchair doing the crossword and living out an uneventful old age.* This was probably the most stupid thing Jimmy had ever done. *Well, maybe not,* he thought. Trusting Norris probably topped that. *Hell, maybe Jimmy was right,* thought Norris. *Maybe me being here was stupid.* Norris stared back at Jimmy.

Jimmy took one more look at Norris, then realising that even more minutes were slipping away, he shut the door of his own car, locked it, then got into the driver's seat of the getaway car in front of Norris. Jimmy turned his head and looked at Norris as he checked behind him, the twitch over his eyebrow still ticking away. “Guess you'd better hang on tight then, puss, I'm late.”

The car splashed onto the road and rounded the corner. Soon they were back on the main road. The traffic had built up and progress was painfully slow. Jimmy peered at his watch. “Now look what you've done.” Tiny beads of sweat gathered on Jimmy's forehead; his neck flushed red. He drummed the steering wheel with his fingers. “Whatever happens, just stay in the car,” said Jimmy, staring at Norris in the rear-view mirror.

Norris had absolutely no intention of letting Jimmy out of his sight. "You complete idiot," meowed Norris. "What have you gone and done. Can't you see where this is heading?"

Jimmy, of course, only heard a long string of meows which he ignored as he worked his way through the gears and headed down the bus lane to a chorus of car horns.

Chapter Twenty

Norris felt himself sliding along the back seat as Jimmy careered down the high street.

"Steady on," meowed Norris.

The car streamed past a pedestrian crossing, throwing a tide of dirty water over a lady waiting to cross, her purple mac clinging to her legs.

"You'll draw attention to yourself," meowed Norris, as he dug his claws into the seat to hang on.

Jimmy looked at the clock on the dashboard. "Shit, shit, shit. Look at the time, they said a quarter past nine, it's gone that already."

"Then don't do it," meowed Norris.

"Quit that wailing," snapped Jimmy. "What the hell am I doing talking to a cat!"

Norris, tired of being thrown around on the back seat, crawled precariously through the gap between the front two seats, over the gear stick and jumped up onto the front passenger seat, next to Jimmy.

"What the..." Jimmy swerved, narrowly missing a car that had pulled out in front of him. With a screech, he slammed his foot on the brakes sending the car into a skid. Norris was thrown forward, crashing against the dashboard.

"Slow down," screeched Norris, but Jimmy was already back on the accelerator. Leaving the driver of the other car dazed, Jimmy ploughed ahead, over the junction and turned left along a street lined with small boutiques and coffee shops and a bingo hall that had clearly once been a cinema. Norris clung to the edge of the seat, his claws now latched into the upholstery, the wipers sweeping hypnotically across the windscreen. Norris could see the clock on the dashboard. Nearly half past nine. This wasn't good. Jimmy wasn't cut out for this kind of thing, but there was nothing Norris could do now to make him change his mind.

Norris remembered that Jimmy had always been a risk taker. Of the unit, he had been the outspoken one, always out in front on manoeuvres, making jokes, carrying his gun with a swagger. But he had been disciplined, they had to be. Those were calculated risks. But this wasn't the same Jimmy that was driving now. This Jimmy Morgan had been ravaged by time, battered by life and now he was acting out of a sense of panic that frankly scared Norris more than their parachute drop into occupied France. Jimmy was displaying an unpredictability that surely could only end in disaster. Norris' stomach curdled and he thought he was going to puke. Jimmy was going to be late and Norris had seen enough movies to know that when a getaway driver is late, all kinds of shit could happen. Only this wasn't a movie, this was real and he was powerless to stop it happening.

The car slowed down. Up ahead, Norris could see a row of shops, their windows misted with condensation, the lights inside ablaze, the doors opening and closing as the first customers of the day ventured from the rain. Norris could see the orange barricades of roadworks on the pavement outside a shop front up ahead. Jimmy indicated to pull over and the car began slowing down further as he manoeuvred. Orange striped cones surrounded what looked like a manhole, two men wearing fluorescent jackets and hard hats were peering into the shop window, their body language fraught. The scruffy burgundy shop sign read:

Razzlers jewellers – established 1925

Jimmy brought the car to a standstill. Despite the hard hats and goggles there was something familiar about the workmen, especially the stout one, his tabard straining across his middle, his arm gesturing wildly at Jimmy. Norris stood up on his hind legs, his paws on the dashboard. The door of the jewellers was open. A stocky man in a crumpled brown suit and trilby was blocking the doorway, an umbrella angled in one hand, a briefcase in the other. As Jimmy threw open the passenger door of the car, a scuffle broke out inside the shop.

The sound of a gun shot rang out. Norris saw the terror in Jimmy's eyes. The man in the suit tossed the umbrella onto the pavement where the wind whipped it into cartwheels along the road. The same man now turned and faced Jimmy, the man's eyes hidden behind dark glasses that dwarfed his face. His hand was pointing straight at Jimmy. In the struggle, the man had lost one of his leather gloves, revealing a set of all too familiar tattoos on his hand.

Frank, thought Norris.

The shop keeper flew out after Frank, grabbing for the briefcase. Frank elbowed him in the face. Jimmy threw open the car door and yanked open the back passenger door. Norris was about to leap out after him when Frank ran towards the car, pushing past Jimmy and went to throw the briefcase on the back seat. It was at this point that things seemed to go into slow motion. In the distance, Norris could hear the sound of sirens. Frank had started to step into the car.

"You're late. What the..." Then he spotted Norris. "It's that bloody cat again...what the..."

Frank paused to stare at the ginger cat sitting on the front passenger seat. The shop keeper, his nose streaming blood, took his chance. He grabbed hold of Frank's legs, pulling him so hard that Frank crashed to the ground, trying in vain to cling onto the door sill. The sirens grew louder. Norris arched his back, all the hairs on his body sprang to attention as though an electric shock was racing through his body. He let out an unearthly "Meoooooow."

Maybe it had been the shock of the gunshot, but Norris could only guess what made Jimmy do what he did next. The shopkeeper wrestled with Frank, who was shouting, the rain pelting the pair of them. Passers-by screamed. The two workmen, who Norris later realised must have been Ernie and the man who had taken to parking outside fifty-four Grantchester Road, ran down a side street and disappeared. Jimmy grabbed his barrel bag from the back of the car and produced a gun. Norris' tail shot out straight behind him, his ears picking up the sound of the police car fast approaching from behind them, its siren pulsating inside his head. A stream of urine soaked into the seat beneath Norris as he saw Jimmy aim the gun at the shopkeeper's head while Frank crawled out of his grasp.

Norris froze. The urine made his fur stick unpleasantly to his legs. He saw before him, Jimmy as a young private, his army uniform brushed with dust, no longer standing in the rain with a gun in his hand, but back in the dank air of the cellar that clogged Norris' throat as urine ran down his leg and into his boot. A gun was pressed cold and hard against his temple, a trickle of sweat smudging his vision. Norris could see Jimmy's blue eyes from behind the pile of crates, the only glint of colour amongst the wooden barrels and sacks that filled the hot cellar, the smell of rancid decay permeating every corner. Jimmy's eyes pleaded with him, but Norris could feel the German soldier's breath on his neck, felt the pressure of metal against his temple. Norris knew he should have been looking for a way out, any advantage he could utilise but instead, all he could see was Jimmy. Norris couldn't stop looking. He couldn't stop his head involuntarily moving in the direction of Jimmy, hidden so nearly completely. But it was too late. A kick to the stomach made Norris crumple to his knees and he felt his arm pointing to Jimmy. Jimmy, who was trapped like a caged rat about to be flushed out. Norris couldn't remember the next few seconds. The pain in his stomach made him wretch but he could hear the animal scream of Jimmy as he was dragged out from his hiding place. It was only then that Norris' instinct had kicked in. He lunged at the leg of the German soldier, pulling him to the ground. Norris noticed the open doorway, temporarily unguarded as Jimmy was dragged into the middle of the cellar. Maybe Jimmy had underestimated Norris' cowardice for he, too, grabbed for the other soldier. But all Norris could focus on was the door and the split second it would take to reach it. He just needed a distraction, anything would do. He knew he should have helped Jimmy, together they may have been able to overpower two soldiers, but for Norris the risk was too high. He saw Jimmy grab for a holstered gun. In that confused second, Norris ran for the door. He heard the shot, out of the corner of his eye he saw the bullet shatter Jimmy's leg but instead of turning back, he kept on running. The sweat running down Norris' face turned once more to rain. Before him, Jimmy still stood with the gun, an old man now, his leg healed but forever crippled, the tremor in his hand making the gun quiver.

Norris streaked out of the car, ignoring the shrieks of the people who had gathered to gawp from the street corner. His heart pounded so violently; Norris thought it would explode. He searched the pavement in that brief moment, taking in the shop door, the open manhole cover beyond the cones, the little girl who was pointing at him, the shop keeper whose eyes bulged as his legs trembled beneath him. Jimmy's hand shook violently as he continued to point the gun. The police car raced along the road towards them. A man in the gathered crowd shouted, “Look, it's a cat!”

Norris ran up Jimmy's legs, along his arm and with his paw, swiped the gun from Jimmy's hand. Taken by surprise, Jimmy spun round to see Norris latched onto his arm, his fur drenched by the rain, sticking up like an angry brush around his face. Frank saw the police car and fled, sprinting down the road, pushing his way through the crowds, darting across the road in front of a lorry, disappearing down an alleyway.

The gun had flown out of Jimmy's hand and across the pavement. In the commotion that followed, the shopkeeper grabbed hold of Jimmy, knocking him to the ground. There Jimmy slumped, his head in his hands, the rain soaking into his trousers. Norris could only look on as a policeman yanked Jimmy up off the pavement, wrenching his arm up behind his back.

Bile rose in Norris' throat as he watched Jimmy being manoeuvred into the waiting car, not as an old man but as a young private, his leg shattered and bleeding, being pulled between two German soldiers and out of Norris' life. Norris had failed him back then and he had failed him again. He felt sick and ashamed, sitting in a puddle of water that seeped up into his very being. A hand grasped him by the scruff of his neck, and he was thrown into the back of a police car and driven away.

Chapter Twenty-One

Well, that was it then, thought Norris, hunched inside a metal cage, its concrete base cold against his belly. The light of a single bulb cast a sickly yellow glow over the shed. A thin scrap of blanket was the only piece of comfort and even that smelt rank. Next to him sat a water bowl in which a fly was doing the back stroke. *So, it looks like I went along for the ride,* thought Norris, *to watch Jimmy Morgan throw away what was left of his life.*

"What yer in 'ere for?"

Norris turned to see a pit bull, its muzzle hard up against the bars of the cage opposite.

"Yer must 'ave done something real bad to end up 'ere."

"Worse than you can possibly imagine," said Norris. *Only I did it twice,* he thought.

"They say animals don't leave the police pound alive, but maybe you could be lucky," said the pit bull. He gulped water from his bowl greedily, turning his back on Norris once again.

"Great," said Norris, tucking his head between his paws.

Minutes turned to hours, the only visitor a police sergeant that scooped unpleasant smelling goo into the dish in front of him. Norris didn't even look up; the smell only soured his mood more. Hours later, the same police sergeant took the pit bull away, pulling him through the door on a length of rope, not letting him finish his last meal.

Norris knew what was likely to be in store for him. This was after all surely some kind of death camp. Well, he deserved it, didn't he? It had been a long time in coming, but as he lay breathing in the stale air, Norris just waited, hoping that now this masquerade of lives would finally come to an end. But Norris couldn't help thinking about Stella. What would happen to her now? Norris knew he should have found a way to stop Jimmy, that he should have done more. But what could he have done? He was stuck inside a stupid cat's body and whatever or whoever was responsible for that charade, must be having a jolly good laugh. Norris missed Stella. And Jimmy? Well, that guilt was devouring him from the inside.

Norris found waiting for death a boring process and he fell asleep huddled in the corner of his cage. He was awoken by the clank of his cage door being opened. The sergeant grabbed him by the scruff of the neck and dropped him into a cat carrier, a very familiar smelling cat carrier.

"Looks like someone wants you after all," said the sergeant, carrying Norris outside.

It was dark and Norris couldn't make out where the sergeant was taking him. A streetlight illuminated a large puddle with an empty fag packet floating across its surface. Then Norris recognised a voice. It was Stella's voice.

"Be careful with him."

"We'll take him from here, thank you." Norris had never been so relieved to hear Mildred's voice.

So it was that Norris found himself once again back on Stella's lap in the back of a car being driven back to fifty-four Grantchester Road. Only this time it wasn't the mini, but a taxicab and Norris knew only too well that Jimmy wasn't going to be there.

"Don't worry," said Stella. Her fingertips stroked Norris' fur through the bars. "I've kept you some bacon and egg from tea."

Mildred was unusually very quiet. She didn't say a word until the taxicab stopped and she thanked the driver. Once indoors, Stella carefully removed Norris from the cat carrier and hugged him tightly. "You must have been so scared," she said. She carried him into the kitchen and set him down by his bowl.

Though Norris' stomach gave a hollow grumble he felt sick, but he didn't have the heart to refuse the bacon that Stella nudged him towards.

"Not as scared as your grandad," said Mildred, as she filled the kettle. "What was he thinking, taking a cat with him...to a robbery of all things. What a stupid, stupid old man he has become." Mildred let the water flow up and over the kettle as she sobbed, her shoulders shaking violently.

"Mum, let me," said Stella, guiding Mildred to a chair and handing her some kitchen towel.

"A robbery...your grandad a getaway driver. I can't believe it! I just can't. His face will be splashed all over the local paper tomorrow. I can't go into work, not with everyone staring and pointing at me, thinking, 'you poor cow.' Oh Dad, you stupid fool!"

Norris finished eating and jumped up onto Stella's lap. He nuzzled her hand. Stella stroked him gently. "Gramps has been acting a bit weird the last couple of weeks and..." She looked down at Norris. "Remember the paper, the story about the robberies, the one he put in the bin?" She looked harder at Norris. "You knew, didn't you?" she said, holding Norris up so that her face looked straight into his. "You tried to tell me, didn't you?"

Mildred blew her nose then stuffed the tissue up her sleeve. "Now, you can stop all that nonsense. Cats can't tell us anything, they can't talk. I'm the one who should have noticed. I should have known. Now look at us, your grandad in prison and us the talk of the town. Oh, my God! When your dad hears about this..."

There was a loud banging on the front door and the telephone began to ring.

"Go away!" shouted Mildred. "Just leave us alone!"

The banging got louder.

"Now remember, Stella, don't open the door to anyone and no answering the phone either. They just want a story and they're not going to get it from me."

Norris curled up in Stella's lap.

"No school for you tomorrow, we best wait until all this dies down," said Mildred. She kissed Stella on the forehead then headed towards the kitchen door.

"What about Gramps?"

"I don't know," said Mildred. "I'm off to bed, don't stay up too late."

Stella scooped up Norris and set him down on the sofa, then turned on the television. The local news was still on and after an interview with a lady in a purple mackintosh, an old picture of Jimmy flashed up on the screen.

"A local pensioner has been arrested in connection with a

string of robberies from jewellery shops. It is the first arrest after a long ongoing investigation. Jimmy Morgan has been remanded in custody, pending trial."

Stella grabbed the remote and flicked over to another channel. Norris stopped watching and curled up beside her. After another knock at the door, Stella turned up the volume.

Chapter Twenty-Two

The next day dragged hopelessly. Mildred spent half the morning on the phone trying to speak to someone, anyone. who could arrange for her to see Jimmy. Norris listened, noting the desperation in her voice. Stella tried and failed to concentrate on her homework. Instead, she made endless cups of tea for Mildred which went undrunk. Despite it being a bright autumnal day, Mildred insisted on keeping the curtains shut lest anyone dared to peer inside. Norris wondered what she was scared of, was it just the nosy neighbours, the persistent reporters or was it being judged by the actions of her father? *And what was Jimmy thinking when he took that gun with him,* thought Norris. Was it even loaded? No matter how Norris played it out in his mind, the scene outside the jewellery shop, he couldn't see how he could have done anything to change it. Maybe he should have tried to crash the getaway car before Jimmy even got there. Yes, maybe that would have been better than this. One leap onto the steering wheel could have made Jimmy swerve and career off course, but it was too late now. The same as it was too late to do anything back in France when he had laid hidden watching from afar, as Jimmy was dragged away by those German soldiers. It was too late to question his actions then and it was too late now. Hell, Jimmy would just have to grass up Frank and Ernie and hope the court would consider leniency. *There was nothing a cat could have done,* thought Norris.

Norris tried to keep Stella company, but she was

distant, plugged into her music, fretting. By the afternoon, Mildred had taken to her bed.

Pushing his way through the curtains in the sitting room, Norris sat on the windowsill. A van had been parked in Grantchester Road most of the morning, with *Piccadilly News* blazoned across its side. A crowd of locals had gathered near the gate of number fifty-four, and they pointed towards the house, towards Norris, the only representative of the family who dared to show their face. Maybe it was time Norris left. After all, what was really keeping him here now? He could walk out that cat flap and go anywhere he wanted to.

Some hours later, Norris watched a young boy open the gate and sidle up the path to the front door. The laces on his trainers had come undone and trailed on the path. He pulled an envelope from his bomber jacket pocket and pushed it through the letterbox. Norris watched him check around to see if anyone had noticed him, the boy then turned, his mouth chewing gum, his hair greasy at the roots, a crop of acne gathering on his cheeks. He headed back to the main road and disappeared. Norris trotted into the hall to find the envelope laying on the mat; a brown, slightly crumpled envelope with Mildred's name written across it in scratchy joined up writing. Norris sniffed it. It smelt of cigarettes.

"What have you got there?" said Stella, heading out of the kitchen. "Mum, there's a note for you."

"Put it in the bin," shouted Mildred from her bed.

"But it might be important," said Stella.

Mildred didn't reply.

Norris rubbed up against Stella's legs, almost

tripping her up as she tried to get through the doorway to the kitchen. "Hey, what are you doing? Get out of the way," she said.

Norris wanted to see that letter. It was important, it had to be or why the messenger? He lifted himself up on his back legs and pawed at Stella's legs.

"Is this what you want?" said Stella, turning the envelope over.

Norris meowed, stretching his paws higher up Stella's leg.

"All right, all right, I'll open it." Stella tore open the envelope and pulled out a thin folded piece of paper. As she read it, she dropped the envelope. Her face slipped into a frown as she seemed to be reading it again.

"You really did want to see this, didn't you?" said Stella, placing the letter onto the kitchen table.

Norris jumped up so he could see it.

"...Jimmy had better not be a grass. No good would come of it. We don't want to have to do anything, after all, we know how important you and Stella are to him."

The letter was unsigned, in the same handwriting as the envelope and it, too, smelt of cigarettes. Stella sat down; all colour bleached from her face. Norris wished he could hug her, tell her everything would be all right, but even if he could, it would have been a lie. It was pretty obvious to him who had written that letter, even if he had underestimated Frank and Ernie. Low level crooks they may be, but desperation had changed them. *Oh, Jimmy,* thought Norris, *now look what you've done.*

After several minutes, Stella picked up the letter,

folded it and slipped it into her back pocket. She scooped Norris up and looked long and hard into his face. "You know more than a cat should," she said. "If I didn't know better, I would say you know more about what's going on here than anyone. But that's just not possible. You're a cat."

Norris meowed, never letting his eyes leave hers.

"What I don't understand is why Gramps took you with him. When I get to see him, that's what I'll ask him." Stella stroke Norris' head.

That night, Norris couldn't settle. He couldn't sleep, he didn't want to. That letter was a threat and Stella knew it. Norris had grown very fond of Stella, more than he cared to admit and maybe, just maybe, he could get through to her enough for her to help him. Upstairs, Norris could hear Mildred talking. More than once he heard Mildred shout. But it was Stella crying that hurt him the most. He had never been one to care much about the hysteria of women. He had very early on in his succession of lives learnt to block out the noise of female tears. His emotional shutters would come down, impenetrable even by the most hysterical wailing. All, that is, except the tears of little Janice. His love for his last daughter was so great that the barrier simply melted away, just as it was doing now, with Stella. Norris knew he couldn't walk away from Stella and abandon her to Frank and Ernie. Something had to be done and that something meant revealing the true culprits in the robberies and catching the ones that got away.

As the clock struck nine o'clock, Norris climbed onto the sitting room windowsill. He felt weary. The wound in his belly was healing, but a heaviness seemed to have sapped all his energy. He knew he needed sleep, yet his brain was wired, fuelled by an edginess he couldn't quite explain. A full moon shone down on Grantchester Road and the cars parked along it. Inside one of them a light flickered, and Norris saw the burning glow of a cigarette. The man was taking pictures, and he was pointing his camera straight at Norris. The last time Norris had seen that man he had been wearing a hard hat and a fluorescent jacket, standing outside the jewellery shop. Norris was sure of it.

Chapter Twenty-Three

And so it was that Norris set out on a new mission, a mission to save Stella. In doing so he may just save Jimmy too, though Norris severely doubted his chances with that one. Stella clearly saw something in Norris which was not just feline. At last, he seemed to be penetrating her scepticism that cats knew nothing and could do nothing. Now it was time to really show her, time was of the essence, but his chief obstacle was Mildred. With her moping around the house, Norris had little chance of getting Stella to realise what was really going on. So, it was fortuitous that, on that second morning, Mildred burst into the sitting room and announced that she had been granted permission to visit Jimmy in prison. She had, she told Stella, to warn him not to turn grass, at least, not yet anyway, until Mildred had sought legal advice.

"Can I come too?" said Stella.

"Absolutely not," said Mildred. "No child of mine is setting foot inside a prison with all those…no, definitely not."

"But I need to see Gramps," said Stella.

Norris sat upright now; his ears pricked. He was sitting on the sitting room windowsill, keeping guard. The car that had been parked outside had left late last night, but an equally suspicious car was parked in its place. Norris didn't recognise the occupant who pretended to be reading the paper for long periods. The edginess Norris had been feeling hadn't left him. It had been playing havoc with his guts.

"Best you stay here. I should be back by late afternoon. The taxi is due in five minutes. I called the school again today to say you were still sick and not to expect you back this week."

"Are you going to tell Gramps about the letter?"

"Yes, of course I am. And I have an appointment to see a solicitor, too. Keep the door locked and don't open it to anyone, do you hear me? No-one. We don't know who we can trust. Not anymore."

Norris meowed at this point. Mildred flashed him a look. "Try to get that cat to go outside today, will you? He's left a dreadful smell in the bathroom this morning. I think he could do with some fresh air."

"What if the police come back?" said Stella.

Norris flinched, his fur ruffling along his back. He recalled yesterday afternoon when two policemen made Mildred let them in. They ransacked Jimmy's bedroom, found his betting slips and the bills. They messed up the sitting room whilst Mildred screamed at them to be careful what they were doing. Thankfully they didn't raise the rug or find the hiding place under the cut floorboard. Norris had sat down firmly on that rug as they searched and washed meticulously, keeping an eye on their movements out of the corner of his eye.

"They have assured me they won't be back," said Mildred, stuffing a fresh handkerchief into her handbag and tying the belt on her beige raincoat. She headed towards the front door and, moments later, left in the taxi.

Norris jumped up onto the sofa next to Stella. Now was his chance to get Stella to realise a few things. He had just crept onto her lap when there was a knock at the front door. Stella flinched. The knock came again, louder this time. Norris ran to the window and peered outside. On the doorstep stood Noreen, a blue floral scarf tied around her head, a savagely crimson lipstick made her pursed lips look even larger than they really were. She knocked again. Stella tried to ignore it. Norris hissed, arching his back. Getting no reply, Noreen peered in through the window and tapped on the glass. Stella jumped up, stood behind Norris and stared back at Noreen. A smile creased across Noreen's face and she gestured to the front door. Norris hissed even louder.

"It's only Noreen," said Stella. "Why are you acting so strangely?" She stroked Norris, trying to calm his fur that now stood in harsh bristles along his back.

"Don't let anyone in," meowed Norris. "You cannot trust them."

Stella went to the door. Norris ran after her meowing, pawing at her legs.

"Stop it, will you," said Stella, as Noreen again knocked on the door. Stella was about to unlock the door when Norris pulled himself up on his hind legs and nipped her leg.

"Ow!" said Stella. "Why did you do that?"

The letterbox rattled and Norris could see Noreen's eyes peering through it. "It's only me, Stella. Noreen."

Norris hissed.

"I thought you might like some company. I didn't want to think of you all alone here."

Stella crouched down to the letterbox and stared back at Noreen. "I'm not alone...what makes you think I am?" said Stella, no longer attempting to open the door.

"I saw your mother leaving in a taxi and thought I might pop in for a cuppa and a chat."

"How convenient," meowed Norris, "you old bag."

"Oh," said Stella. She raised her hand to the lock again. This time Norris leapt up, patting Stella's hand with his paw, his claws extended. "Stop that will you," said Stella.

"Who are you talking to?" said Noreen.

"Our cat and…"

"Did you say cat…that ginger cat?"

"Look, I'm fine, really, thank you," said Stella, pushing Norris' paw away.

Sensing a victory, Norris walked into the kitchen, his tail held high. Stella followed, leaving Noreen crouched by the letterbox. When further attempts to convince Stella to open the door went unanswered, Noreen eventually gave up and, pleased with his success, Norris rubbed up against Stella's legs and purred loudly.

"So, you don't like Noreen," said Stella. "Well neither do I but…"

Norris stiffened. He arched his back again and let out a piercing hiss.

"You really don't like Noreen do you…and something makes me think I should listen to you. Mum did say not to let anyone in."

Norris purred again and wove in and out of Stella's legs. This communicating lark was getting exhausting. If only Norris could think of another way.

Stella flipped the cat flap. "Why not take a walk," she said.

Norris ignored her. Stella picked him up and tried to encourage him out of the cat flap head-first. "I might not be able to go outside but you can," she said.

Norris reversed back inside and sprinted across the kitchen out of Stella's reach.

"Okay, you win."

Norris knew they didn't have much time without Mildred. He trotted back over to Stella, rubbed against her legs then ran out of the kitchen and up the stairs.

"You want me to follow you, don't you?" said Stella, catching up with Norris on the stairs.

Norris led her into Jimmy's bedroom. Mildred had restored order in there, she had even changed the bedding as she said the room felt violated. Norris walked over to the rug and with his head to the floor he tried to lift the edge of it, his bottom stuck up in the air.

"What are you doing?" said Stella.

Norris managed to turn the edge of the rug over with his paw and bit down on the corner. Walking backwards he tried to pull the rug out of the way. *How could one thin rug be so heavy*, he thought.

"What are you trying to show me?" said Stella, taking the rug from Norris' mouth. "You are trying to show me something, aren't you?"

Norris meowed.

Stella pulled back the rug. "There's nothing here," she said.

Norris attacked the cut edge of the floorboard with his paw, scrabbling furiously.

"Oh, I see now," said Stella. She crouched down and prised up the floorboard. Underneath, there sat the money, still rolled up with an elastic band, but the gun was missing. All that remained was the box of bullets. When Stella opened it, they were all present and correct. So, the gun wasn't loaded after all, thought Norris.

Stella sat on the end of the bed. Norris saw a tear run down her cheek. He jumped up beside her and gently rubbed against her.

"Oh, what has Gramps done? How could he?"

Chapter Twenty-Four

It was nearly mid-morning and what had Norris accomplished other than to upset Stella more? So, he had shown her that Jimmy was a crook, but as he was in prison, Stella knew that already. Norris had tried to show Stella that Noreen wasn't to be trusted but he couldn't explain why. This was just so infuriating. Cats couldn't talk, everybody knew that. So, what could he do?

Stella put the money and bullets back under the floorboard and rolled the rug back into place. She looked out of the window. Norris jumped up to look but the car, even if it had been suspicious, was gone. Those people who were walking along Grantchester Road seemed to be going about their day-to-day business. Even the news van hadn't arrived that day.

"I wonder how Gramps is," said Stella, hugging Norris. "It must be horrid to be locked up."

You could say that again, thought Norris. Being locked up seemed to be becoming a bit of a habit, and not in a good way.

"He should just tell the police everything he knows," added Stella.

Part of Norris agreed. From what he'd seen of Frank and Ernie, the 'threat' could well be just that; but the third man, well, Norris couldn't be sure, but he didn't like the look of him at all and if anyone was the mastermind of this little outfit, it was him.

"Mum will make Gramps tell her what happened, you wait and see," said Stella, squeezing Norris against her.

Norris wasn't so sure.

Stella disappeared downstairs and curled up on the sofa to read a book. Norris needed to find a better way to communicate with her, but he just couldn't think how. He trotted into Stella's room. On the floor, he found Stella's open school bag. He nudged out a notebook and with his paw managed to flip open a page. A bit of rummaging and he had located a pen and patted it across the floor. It soon became very evident to Norris that without an opposing thumb there was no way he could get a hold of it. In his efforts, the pen rolled away under the bed. Having retrieved it, and with a generous coating of dust now adhering to the top of his head, Norris grabbed the pen in his mouth but try as he might, he couldn't get the pen the right way round to write with using his mouth. He had seen limbless artists who had painted with their mouth but every time he tried to angle the pen down, he dropped it. His paws were useless to help, it was like trying to hold a pen in a hand that was strapped in a bandage. In frustration, Norris bit down with his teeth until the pen shattered, leaving his mouth full of plastic shards. Well, that proved it. Cats couldn't write either. So, what the hell could they do?

Of course, Norris had spoken too soon about the news van. He headed downstairs to find something to eat when there was a knock at the door and the letterbox rattled. Running into the sitting room, Norris put his head through the curtain to see who it was. A bright light flashed in his eyes as a photographer pointed a camera at him through the window. He was joined by a young woman holding a big fuzzy microphone.

Several more reporters were sprinting up the path, notebooks at the ready.

"Who's there?" said Stella. She joined Norris at the window and peered through the curtain. Again, the camera flashed. "I think they're rather interested in you," said Stella, pulling the curtain shut again and scooping Norris up. "If you will take centre stage at a robbery, what do you expect?"

Again, the letterbox rattled. Norris struggled until Stella had to let him down. He ran into the hall and sat on the door mat. Someone prised open the letterbox and looked straight at him. "Why did Jimmy Morgan take your cat to a robbery?" called the voice of a man.

Stupid reporter, thought Norris. Jimmy didn't do any such thing, but Norris doubted they could ever imagine the real story.

"Come away," said Stella, pulling Norris towards her. "Go away," she shouted through the letterbox. "Leave us alone."

Norris and Stella camped out in the sitting room for several hours whilst the media frenzy continued outside. Stella, close to tears by now, called Mildred on her mobile. "Mum, there are reporters outside and they won't leave us alone. They keep trying to take our picture. They want to know why Gramps took a cat with him to the robbery." Stella pulled the curtains even tighter together, pushing Norris onto the floor. "Of course I won't let him go outside, Mum, I've barricaded the cat flap."

"Don't bother locking me in," meowed Norris. "I have no intention of going out there."

Just to check, Norris ran up the stairs and peered

through the curtains in Stella's room. Sure enough, a reporter was in the garden, another sitting on the fence at the back. *We're surrounded,* thought Norris.

"When will you be home?" said Stella. She sat curled up on the sofa, cuddling a cushion as Norris headed back into the sitting room. "Okay, but please hurry. I'm scared, Mum. What if they try to get in?"

And so, they waited. Surrounded by the press, desperate for a story. Norris could only imagine the picture that would appear on the front page of the newspaper tomorrow. Fame at last, but not in the way Norris had once hoped for. Three lives ago, he had auditioned and got the part of the lead in a play to be performed at the Theatre Royal in Cricklington. Norris had had great expectations, but just before opening night he had got into a fight which left him with a black eye and a thick lip. The understudy opened that night, and Norris was forced to admit that he wasn't cut out for the stage after all. And now he was a celebrity, it would seem. But for what? For trying to stop a stupid old man throwing away what life he had left. Just brilliant.

Norris was contemplating the tuna in his bowl when Mildred arrived home. She swept into the hall slamming the door shut behind her. "Stella, are you alright? I really did mean to be home earlier. I can only imagine what you've had to put up with having that lot camped outside."

Mildred slung her bag on the hall table, pulled off her raincoat and collapsed into a kitchen chair. She kicked off her patent black court shoes and wiggled her toes, pink painted nails visible through her tights. "Put the kettle on, will you, love. I could do with a brew."

"How's Gramps?"

"He surprisingly had very little to say."

"But he is alright, isn't he?"

"He looked old, pale I thought, and he had some kind of bruise over his eye. I asked him how he got it, and he just told me not to fuss, you know what he's like."

Seeing the look on Stella's face, Norris let the last mouthful drop out of his mouth. He jumped up onto Stella's lap.

"He is going to be okay, isn't he, Mum?"

Okay, thought Norris. *Okay?* The way things were developing, Norris certainly doubted it. A bruise, she said. Norris could only imagine how that had happened, but he had a horrible feeling Frank and Ernie were involved somehow.

Mildred clasped her hands around her mug. "Yes…well, I hope so. I asked your grandad why he did it and he just shrugged. Anyone would have thought I'd asked him what he wanted for his tea. He was involved in a robbery, part of a criminal gang, so the police say. Not just a getaway driver, but party to a conspiracy to commit a robbery, an armed robbery. He had a gun! I can't believe it…I just can't…and to top it all, he took a cat with him…a bloody cat, of all things." Mildred pointed at Norris. "That bloody cat…why…why did he do it? How could he?" Mildred pushed away her mug, letting the tea slop over the side. She slumped onto the table, her head in her hands.

"Don't cry, Mum, please."

Norris felt a lump of tuna stick in his throat.

"Mum, what did the solicitor say?"

Mildred looked up; her mascara smudged across her cheek in a dirty streak. "He says that unless your grandad co-operates with the police and helps them convict the rest of the gang, he's likely to go to prison for a very long time. The fact he is an old man doesn't seem to come into it. Armed robbery, they're calling it."

"But what about the letter?" said Stella.

Mildred sniffed. "I don't know. I really don't. I'm so sorry, Stella. I really thought leaving your dad and coming here would give us a new start, a chance to build a new life."

Norris couldn't listen to anymore. How could he? He couldn't watch Stella cry. He crept away and crawled under the chair in the sitting room, putting his paw over his nose, wishing he could sleep but knowing he most definitely would not.

Chapter Twenty-Five

Next morning, Norris really was on the front page of the newspaper. It was a far from flattering picture of him, a scrawny ginger cat poking his head through the blue curtains of fifty-four Grantchester Road.

"Ex veteran takes his cat to jewellery heist."

Really, what nonsense those papers printed; he thought. A bungled smash and grab could never be described as a heist and poor Jimmy had no idea Norris was there until it was too late to do anything about it.

Stella looked at the pictures in disbelief. "Do I really have to go to school today, Mum?"

Mildred scraped butter across her toast. Her foundation barely concealed the bags under her eyes. "Best get back to normal, whatever that is. It's got to be better than sitting around here all day being gawped at."

Norris lapped the last of the yolk from the fried egg in his bowl and set about washing the drips from his whiskers.

"They'll do worse than gawp at me at school, Mum. They'll...well, they will. I know they will."

"I'm sorry, love, but if you don't face them now it will only get worse and if I don't get back to work, they'll sack me, and then where will we be? We need the money. That solicitor cost me a week's wages."

Norris could imagine the taunts. He knew only too well how cruel children could be. Mildred opened the front door to let Stella through. The word 'scum' had been sprayed over the front door crudely with green aerosol.

Norris watched Stella leave, trailing reluctantly behind Mildred. He had been tempted to follow her, but he didn't want to make the situation any worse, after all, he was a notorious celebrity now and anyway, he had something he needed to do.

Norris wanted to pay Noreen a visit. He was sure Frank and Ernie would be lying low after the robbery fiasco, but something told Norris that Noreen would have wanted to stay put. Pushing his way through the cat flap, Norris checked the coast was clear, then made his way down the garden and up onto the fence at the bottom. Thankfully, there was no sign of Boris, maybe the reporters had scared him away for now. Norris prayed there wouldn't be a reporter on the track below him, he doubted he could control himself if there was and he had no desire to see the inside of the police pound again.

A pale sun tried to squeeze through the clouds as Norris made his way to Hawthorne Rise, trying not to draw attention to himself but few people were out and about and those that were, ignored him. Maybe the reporters had grown tired and moved on to a new story. Norris was glad not to have to run as his legs felt heavy that morning, weighted with fatigue. His head was fuzzy still, with an edginess that he couldn't shake off. He reached the pebble dashed bungalow and concealed by the long grass, he crept up to the windowsill of the living room and peered beyond the row of cacti. It was empty, not even a mug on the coffee table. Norris peered closer and could just see through the open door inside. Only one coat hung in the hall and that looked to belong to Noreen, its burgundy wool a little tattered on the bottom, one purple glove sticking out of the pocket. So, Norris jumped down and skirted round the bungalow for signs of life. The dining room was also empty. A lumpy corduroy dog bed lay next to the radiator but there was no sign of the terrier. In the kitchen, one mug stood upside down on the draining board next to a bowl and spoon. Just as he thought, Noreen had been left to hold the fort whilst Frank lay low, most probably with Ernie somewhere. The only light shone in the bathroom. Sitting on the narrow window ledge, Norris could hear the shower running.

When Norris re-traced his footsteps back down Hawthorne Rise, he couldn't help feeling disappointed. What had he expected to find? A jewellery stash on display? Frank counting out a pile of notes? Noreen wouldn't be stupid enough to have anything incriminating in the bungalow and Frank, a fugitive, would be hiding somewhere else. The police may publicly have said they had no leads on the other gang members, but Frank was acting scared, that much was obvious. Only time would tell what Jimmy would decide to do. And Norris, what could he do? Norris knew that despite every odd stacked against him, in fact barricading him into a corner, he had to find a way to tell Stella about Frank. If he could only do that, then maybe, just maybe, she would help him. Because the way Norris saw it now, this life, this sick excuse of a life, was a punishment and unless he did something, Norris would be forced to watch Jimmy live out his days in prison, knowing he probably helped put him there.

Norris had very nearly made it back to fifty-four Grantchester Road when a car screeched to a halt beside him. Hearing a door open and footsteps, Norris went to run but a hand grabbed his tail. Norris found himself being dragged back down the pavement, the pain in his tail causing a burning sensation in his nether regions.

"Gotcha," said a voice, a voice that made Norris' fur ping to attention.

Norris twisted round. The hand, its chubby fingers clenched tightly around his tail, belonged to the third man. Norris recognised his tiny dark eyes, like raisins sunken into an overproved bun. His middle bulged against an anorak that strained to contain it. Norris hissed, long and hard.

"Achoo." The sneeze was followed by another, then another. Norris screeched and lashed out with his claws so frantically and with such precision that soon a drip of blood ran down the man's hand, his eyes shrinking deeper into his face. But no matter how fiercely Norris struggled, his claws spread out, sweeping the air, he couldn't free himself.

"Put him down," screamed another voice. Stella's voice. Then more voices joined in.

"Stop him, someone."

"Call the police."

Stella grabbed hold of Norris' front paws and pulled. Norris thought he might be torn in two until, in a panic, the man, now uncontrollably sneezing, let go of Norris' tail, jumped back into his car and sped off. Stella clasped Norris to her and watched the car, far in excess of the speed limit, being pursued by a young man on a bicycle.

"Is the cat all right?" A woman had stopped to help. She put down her string shopping bag, bulging with tins, and gently stroked the top of Norris' head. "How could anyone do something like that?" she said. Then the woman looked more closely at Norris. "Isn't that the cat from the robbery?" she said. "I'm sure it is. I saw the picture in the paper."

"No," said Stella. "I think you must be mistaken. I'm sorry, but I have to go now."

Stella, still clutching Norris tightly, walked through the gate of number fifty-four and let herself in, trying not to notice the graffiti on the front door.

"Scum!" called a girl behind them, leaning over the wall. "About right, I reckon."

Norris didn't get to have a good look at her. Stella pushed the door closed behind them and hugged Norris so tight he thought his ribs might crack.

Chapter Twenty-Six

Surely it wasn't lunchtime already, thought Norris, as he allowed Stella to continue squeezing him. When at last she released him, Norris looked up at the clock on the sitting room mantelpiece to see that it was only shortly after eleven. Stella slumped onto the sofa and clicked on the television. A morning chat show appeared, though Stella seemed more interested in the magazine she began reading than the droning voices from the screen. Norris wished he could ask Stella what had happened, though he could well imagine himself. He remembered the one time he had joined a group of boys as they taunted another called Frederick. It was many lives ago now, but Norris could still recall how awkward he felt. No part of him wanted to be involved but making a stand would only have increased his chances of being the next victim. Norris had yet to have gained a sense of individual determination, that would come later. The look on Frederick's face as he tried to dodge down an alley, pursued by threats that ricocheted after him, stayed with Norris for many days afterwards.

During his lives, if Norris' own children had been bullied, he wasn't aware of it. His selfishness and self-absorption had kept him on the periphery of his family's lives and only since his beloved Janice was born had he come to realise too late what he had missed; the pride that went with parenthood. He wondered what Mildred would do if Stella told her the truth, but who was he to judge?

Norris grew restless, impatient. Any novelty factor in being a cat had evaporated along with his patience. Whilst Jimmy sat in prison awaiting trial, Mildred would be left trying to find a way to pay the bills. Did Jimmy even own this house or was there a mortgage or rent to be paid? *It wouldn't be long*, thought Norris, *before Stella and Mildred could face losing their new home altogether*. Some sanctuary this place had turned out to be. Despite wanting to walk away, as he always had when times proved difficult, Norris knew he couldn't abandon Stella. So, like it or not, he had to find a way. The 'third man', as Norris decided to think of him, was prowling. Why? To capture a cat, most unlikely. That left the only explanation for why a fugitive would be in Grantchester Road, and that was Stella. A knot grew in Norris' belly, his edginess had not been wrong. That note was no idle threat then, which meant Jimmy needed more persuading to ensure he kept quiet. There was no way Norris, as a cat, could follow a car and he still had no idea who the 'third man' was. Only Frank could lead Norris to him.

Having paced around the house for long enough, Norris trotted back into the sitting room. Stella was gone, leaving the television babbling away to an empty sofa. The fur on Norris' back rippled, that edginess escalating. So preoccupied with the 'third man', he allowed panic to rear its head. Running into the hall, Norris looked in the kitchen, but Stella wasn't there. He raced up the stairs, so fast he skidded on the landing as he rounded the corner to Stella's room, but he found that empty, too. Norris couldn't hear anything. Where could she be? The tremor in his legs made him stumble as he headed for Jimmy's bedroom and nudged open the door. To his relief, he found Stella sitting on the side of the bed. Spread out across the duvet was the newspaper that must have been delivered that morning, though Norris hadn't noticed it. The paper was open at a double page spread with a picture of Jimmy, not as he was now, but as a young private, newly conscripted, tall and slender in his uniform, leant up against a gate post. Norris scanned the headline:

"...Man arrested in connection with jewellery heist was prisoner of war."

Stella sat very still. She had a black and white photograph of her grandad in her hands. The bureau drawers were open, clearly Stella had been looking for something. Tears pooled in her eyes and dripped onto the photograph in her hands.

So, the press hadn't moved on, they had been digging and what they had unearthed made Norris' mouth run dry, his skin to shiver all over. Plagued by guilt that had never left him, Norris had blocked out what might have happened to Jimmy Morgan that day after Norris had furtively watched him being dragged away by German soldiers. That their mission in occupied France, which started as an adventure for two inexperienced and naïve young men, could end in such a way because of an error of judgement fuelled by cowardice. Norris' cowardice. Norris had escaped France, it had taken a long time, and it wouldn't have been possible without the courage of others, a courage that he himself just couldn't muster when he needed it most. Back in England, Norris had tried to wipe the memories from his consciousness. When Jimmy had been reported missing in action, Norris' account was minimal and lacking. He pushed forward with his life, never looking back, though the guilt tinged everything he did for years to come. Now Norris was forced to see that reality in Stella's tears. He felt ashamed. Jimmy had been a comrade, but he also considered him a friend, some friend Norris had turned out to be.

Norris' guess was that Mildred didn't know this one awful fact about her father. Clearly, neither did Stella before today. Norris knew that journalists liked to dig for nuggets, anything to sell a story but surely this would take more than digging. *Noreen,* thought Norris. *Would she?* Would she sell a family secret for a cash return? Of course she would. Maybe she couldn't resist a little money of her own now Frank was out of the way, though Norris doubted Frank would be happy about it.

Stella put out her hand and stroked Norris. The open drawer of the bureau was full of papers, small cardboard wallets and snippets of Jimmy's life. Norris walked over to it and peered inside. He nudged the contents with his nose.

"Anyone would think you were looking for something,' said Stella, kneeling down beside him and lifting him onto her lap. Norris kept rooting.

"Careful," said Stella, as Norris flipped a small envelope, yellowed with age, out of the drawer. It fell, a flutter of small black and white photographs scattering on the floor beside them.

"Now look what you've done," said Stella, reaching to pick them up.

Norris looked at the pictures and, in amongst a handful of images of Jimmy, was a picture of his unit. Grainy and a little crumpled, Norris recognised himself, standing next to Jimmy. They looked like they had been talking to one another, maybe sharing a joke. Norris put his paw on the photograph and let out a high-pitched meow. He wanted so much for Stella to know that that was him, Norris. But how could she ever know that? How could she ever connect a ginger cat with a red-haired private in a black and white photograph, taken a lifetime ago?

"That's Gramps," said Stella, holding up the picture for a closer look.

"Yes," meowed Norris, "And that's me. Me, I say!"

Stella pushed Norris away and gathered up the pictures. She slipped them back into the envelope and returned it to the drawer, closing it gently.

Norris wondered why Jimmy had kept it all those years. For a lifetime, Norris feared Jimmy must have felt betrayed. Maybe he even hated Norris. Seeing the picture of them together, unaware of the terrors that lay before them, he felt a sadness that swelled inside him, turning his legs to deadened stone. If cats could cry, he would be crying now. Leaving Stella, he slunk out of Jimmy's room and retreated back down to the sitting room, back under the chair. Curled tightly in a ball, Norris put one paw over his eyes and not for the first time he wished he could die.

Chapter Twenty-Seven

Norris woke to the sound of a man's voice in the hall. A voice he didn't recognise. He heard the front door close and Stella talking softly, too softly for Norris to hear what she was saying. His fur prickled. Arching his back and shaking himself awake, he sprinted into the hallway in time to see Stella sit down at the kitchen table opposite a middle-aged man, ruffled jeans concealing his white trainers, a blue polyester sports fleece, unzipped, a sprinkling of raindrops on the shoulders. The man's face had a ruddy glow, as if he had been running. Tousled brown hair, a shade too long, rubbed on his collar and flecks of grey hair sprouted behind his ears.

Norris trotted into the kitchen, his whiskers taut, his stomach nauseous, his eyes planted on Stella, who had pulled the cuffs of her school jumper over her hands, one thumb now pushed through a rough hole, her teeth chewing her bottom lip.

"Dad, I'm okay, really."

The tension caught in Norris' throat dropped, his ears now drawn back as he watched the two of them tiptoeing around each other. So this was Greg, the womaniser who drove Mildred back to Jimmy.

"You can't stay here, not now," said Greg, playing with the edge of a raffia table mat, his nails bitten down to the quick, the taint of nicotine on his skin.

"I'll call Mum, you should talk to her," said Stella.

"Just come home, until this has blown over. It would be for the best."

"Dad, it won't just blow over, Gramps is in prison. He needs us."

"Like hell he does." Greg tossed the mat over and pushed back his chair. "He's an armed robber. When are you going to realise you shouldn't be here, mixed up in all this. Have you seen what's written on the front door?"

"But Dad…"

"Grab your things, we can go now. I'll call your Mum later."

"No," said Stella. "I won't leave Mum, not after what you did to her."

The colour seeped out of Greg's cheeks. He stood, his hands clutching the back of his chair. "That's adult stuff, you don't understand, and anyway, I'm still your dad."

"Well maybe you should have thought about that when…"

Greg pushed a hand through his hair, its thinning strands now erect tufts on his head, stiffened by gel into a rakish sculpture.

"I'm sorry…okay…is that what you want me to say. It's complicated."

"Yeah well, I'm staying. I'm all Mum has now."

A tear glistened on Stella's cheek. She scrubbed it away with her sleeve, smearing her eyeliner, smudging it across her mottled cheek.

Norris weaved around her legs, purring. He couldn't bear to see her pain. He tried to stroke her as he used to stroke his daughter, Janice, when she cried.

"Is that the cat?" Greg bent down towards Norris, reaching out to touch his back.

Norris ruffled his fur and flicked his tail. He glared back at Greg, daring him to touch him.

"That's quite some celebrity you have there. Why did your grandad take it to the robbery with him?"

Stella scooped Norris up and put him on her lap. She stroked him gently. "He's my cat and…I don't know. I don't know why Gramps took him, it makes no sense at all, none of this does."

Greg sat down. "Maybe I could stay for a bit, talk to your Mum when she gets back. I could pop out and get us something to eat, would you like that?"

"Yeah, I haven't eaten today, I…"

"You look pale. I'll get us fish and chips, I know how much you love that, with extra vinegar, as always."

Greg rose. He put a hand on Stella's shoulder. Norris could feel her hand trembling on his fur.

"I'll be back in twenty minutes. Why don't you pop the kettle on."

As the front door closed, Stella's sobs filled the space Greg had left behind.

Stella popped the last soggy chip into her mouth. She hunted in the batter for the last flakes of cod and fed them to Norris.

"How's school?" Greg scrunched up his empty chip wrapper and tossed it into the pedal bin, the flap clattering shut.

"You know, okay, I guess," said Stella.

"You don't sound so sure. Your Mum should have kept you out of school. It's not right you having to deal with this."

"Just leave it, Dad, all right? If it wasn't this, it would

be something else. Nobody likes the new kid in class. I hate school anyway."

"I told your Mum you should have stayed with me, it's not right to change schools at your age."

Stella pushed her cold tea away and hugged Norris tightly. "Why would I have wanted to stay with you…with her around…with you two…"

"Yeah well, she's gone. She got bored and left, so I'm on my own."

Norris heard a key in the front door. He pricked up his ears, listening to Mildred close the door behind her, hang up her coat and toss off her shoes.

"Well, I can't say I'm sorry, Dad."

"What do you think you're doing here?" Mildred stood in the kitchen doorway, uncurling a silk scarf from around her neck.

"I…"

"Well, think again. It's time you were leaving." Mildred screwed the scarf into a ball in her fist and thrust her handbag onto the work surface next to the kettle. A teaspoon skittered to the floor.

"I came to see my daughter, to make sure she's all right."

"To take her away more like. Stella, go to your room."

"But Mum, I'm not going anywhere."

"Too right, you're not. And take that cat with you, that sodding cat is all I've heard about at work all day."

Mildred glared at Norris. He pulled himself up on Stella's lap, his fur stiffened, his green eyes stared right back at her.

"If only you could talk, you stupid thing," said Mildred, waving her finger at Norris. Norris narrowed his eyes. "Maybe then we'd have some idea of what's going on around here."

"Don't think I haven't tried," meowed Norris, in a long stream of expletives. "Maybe if I could then finally, I could make a difference around here."

"And you can stop that caterwauling, or I'll take you right back to that rescue centre."

Stella gasped, squeezing Norris tightly to her chest, clamping her hands over his ears.

"Just get that cat out of my sight. My head feels like its trapped in the jaws of a nutcracker, any more of that…noise…and it will crack open."

"Sit down Mildred, I'll make you a brew. Stella, best do as your Mum says."

"Oh no, you don't," said Mildred. "Don't go thinking you can make yourself at home here. You made your bed, so go and lie in it."

"She left him, Mum," said Stella, cradling Norris.

"Well, don't go thinking I'm about to climb straight back in. To your room Stella, now!"

Upstairs, Norris settled on Stella's windowsill, the glass cool against his fur, the road outside quiet in the wake of evening. Stella sat hunched at the end of her bed, listening to the row that escalated downstairs, punctuated every few seconds by Mildred's shrill voice, as cupboards banged in sympathy.

Norris was exhausted. What sleep he had managed in the last few days had been restless, driven by nightmares. A cold draft made him shiver. He jumped onto Stella's bed and curled up on her pillow, putting one paw over his eyes. Stella turned the pages of a novel, thought her eyes surely couldn't have read the words through their veil of tears.

The sound of breaking glass woke Norris. A shower of splinters rained down on the windowsill and carpet. Norris spun round. Stella dropped her book. The house brick came to rest on top of Stella's slippers, a note strapped around it with an elastic band.

Chapter Twenty- Eight

"Jimmy had better keep his mouth shut"

The words were formed of letters, each cut from newspaper print and glued roughly in place.

Norris had wanted to see who had thrown it but Stella had scooped him up from the bed, wrapping her arms around his struggling legs, clenching him tightly under one arm. A damp breeze buffeted the curtains as the wind caught on the jagged glass.

Mildred appeared first, followed by Greg, who pushed in front to snatch the note from Stella's hand.

"This isn't the first, is it?" he said.

"No." Mildred sank to the bed, her shoulders sagged.

"Who's sending them?" Greg looked from Mildred to Stella.

Stella shrugged.

Mildred let a strangled sigh escape her before burying her head in her hands.

Norris let out a piercing meow, but shrieking Frank and Ernie's names only made Mildred's sigh escalate into an inhuman moan.

"Get that cat out of here before I strangle it!" Greg put a tentative hand on Mildred's shoulder.

Norris saw her push Greg's hand away before Stella whisked Norris out of the room and carried him downstairs. Behind them, he heard the sound of broken glass being gathered together accompanied by the sobs of Mildred.

Squirming fiercely, Norris managed to escape Stella's

hold, and he ran across the hall and headed into the sitting room. He pounced up onto the windowsill and scanned Grantchester Road. There was no sign of that car parked outside, just the headlights of a trickle of traffic as dusk muffled everything outside. Norris thought he saw a coated figure at the end of the road, standing by a streetlight, beyond its amber glow, and what looked like the tip of a lit cigarette, a tiny speck in the growing gloom. But then it, too, was swallowed.

Footsteps thundered down the stairs and burst into the sitting room.

"We need to call the police," said Greg, hanging onto the door frame, "but your Mum won't hear of it."

"What about Gramps?" said Stella, standing next to Norris now, leaning up against the windowsill, her fingers playing with a small hole in her woolly tights. "Mum says he won't say who was with him as it would only make things worse."

"I don't think it's up to your grandad now, is it? This is intimidation, just look at the state of your mother."

"But Mum says someone in prison hit Gramps, that he…"

"Don't expect me to feel sorry for him. It's armed robbery for Christ's sake, he had a gun. If I'd known he was dangerous as well as stupid I'd have…"

"You'd have what, Dad, stopped us leaving you? Gramps is kind, he wouldn't hurt anyone. There must have been a mistake."

"Yeah well, I doubt your Nan would have agreed…"

"But…" Stella's voice crumbled. Norris felt more useless than ever. As useless as when he watched Irene wail as Janice's tiny coffin was lowered into the ground. He couldn't find the words then and now, now all he could say was meow and what good was that? He rubbed himself up against Stella, his rhythmic purr competing against the tears that fell repeatedly, forcing their way out as Stella leant against Norris, the hole in her tights gaping wide.

"You can't stay here, not now."

"But Dad..."

"We're not going anywhere, not with you."

Norris looked up. Mildred walked into the room and lowered herself into Jimmy's chair. She picked up the paisley cushion and hugged it. Her mascara painted black streaks down her cheeks. One of her pencilled eyebrows had been erased making her look lopsided. Her hair had collapsed into a clump on her head, its grey roots sticking straight up from her forehead. She cradled the cushion, one slipper-less foot on top of the other, a hot pink painted toenail sticking through her nylon stockings.

"And don't go calling the police, neither. I promised Dad, I wouldn't get them involved. I'll go and see him, if I can."

"You stupid bitch!"

Greg slammed the sitting room door behind him.

Norris sat on the rug in the middle of the floor between Mildred and Stella, the only two important things Jimmy had left. Norris had never coped well with crying women. He usually resorted to walking away until they got whatever it was out of their system and some sort of normality resumed. Now, Norris was torn between doing just that and doing the right thing. *But what the hell,* thought Norris, *was the right thing,* and even if he did know what that was, how could a cat do it? So, instead, Norris did nothing. He curled up into a tight ball on the chair by the windowsill and pretended to sleep, even though that was never likely to happen.

When Mildred and Stella finally went upstairs together, Norris found himself having to share the sitting room with Greg. Norris kept his eyes tightly shut and didn't move a hair whilst Greg made up a bed on the sofa. Only when Greg had turned out the light did Norris dare open an eye. Greg sprawled across the sofa, one leg dangling on the floor, the quilt barely containing his backside. There were no sounds from Mildred or Stella upstairs; just the snuffled snore from the sofa joined the ticking of the clock on the mantelpiece.

Pushing through the velvet curtains, Norris took up his vigil on the windowsill. Under the streetlamp a young man stopped to let his dog cock its leg. A lone car drove past, its headlights sweeping the otherwise empty pavement. A slice of moon hung above Grantchester Road. Norris felt his eyes droop and he collapsed into a deep sleep.

It wasn't the finger of sunlight that woke Norris next morning, but Mildred's scream.

"Stella's gone!"

Chapter Twenty-Nine

Norris raced up the stairs, darting through the gap between Greg's legs as he neared the landing. Inside the room that Mildred and Stella shared the broken window was ajar, the curtain flapping in a stiff breeze. Mildred stood dressed in just a flannelette nightie which was covered with tiny purple violets, her cheeks still smudged with mascara from the night before. Norris froze in the doorway as he took in Stella's empty bed, the duvet in a heap at one end. Greg pushed past Norris, nudging him roughly with his foot.

"Gone? She can't just have gone!" he shouted, thrusting his head out of the window, knocking loose fragments of glass onto his bare feet. "Where were you? You must have heard something? Did she..."

Mildred wailed. "Someone's taken her, I know they have, or why else would the window latch be broken..."

"But you were here," snapped Greg. "You'd have seen them, stopped them..."

"Well, I didn't hear them, did I?" shrieked Mildred. "I'd taken one of my sleeping pills, hadn't I...after last night...after that note and..." Mildred collapsed onto Stella's bed, clutching Stella's pillow tightly to her chest.

"You should never have come here," said Greg, raking his fingers through his hair.

"Well, you're to blame for that," sobbed Mildred.

So, the note hadn't been a threat, it was a warning of what was to come. Frank and Ernie were behind this, knowing Mildred would tell Jimmy, so they really didn't trust Jimmy not to talk.

Greg headed to the door.

"Where are you going?" sobbed Mildred.

"To do what you should have done already, call the police," he yelled, running down the stairs.

"But you can't!" screamed Mildred. "They might hurt her."

Norris chased Greg, down the stairs, along the hall, through the kitchen. Then Norris darted out of the cat flap. The sharp morning air caught his lungs. They could have taken Stella anywhere, but he couldn't just sit and watch Mildred and Greg tear into each other. Even if they did call the police, the police would have no idea where to start.

Norris sniffed beneath Stella's window which looked out over the back garden. Sure enough, the grass was flattened just there and something, probably the legs of a ladder, had dug into the mud. Whoever took Stella must have come through the garden and sure enough the door set in the back wall had been left open slightly, as it now banged in the sharp wind which chilled Norris' ears. With a deft poke of his paw, he managed to swing it open long enough to nip through it and onto the track beyond. There were tyre marks in the mud and what looked like one large boot print. Frank and Ernie's gang may be criminals but pretty careless ones at that. They'd left behind enough evidence to keep the police busy. It had rained in the night and Norris had to skirt around large puddles as he made his way along the track and back to Grantchester Road. Mud squelched between his toes, and he shivered, the wind rippling along his fur, seeking out the flesh beneath. He stopped on the pavement outside number fifty-four and wondered what to do. There was no way Noreen would have Stella at the bungalow, so Norris headed off towards the lock up garage. The vehicle which would have had to carry Stella, and a collapsible ladder had to be stowed somewhere, and it was as good a place to start as any.

Why did they have to take Stella? She'd shown him such kindness when he didn't deserve it, and now she was gone, and he hadn't heard a thing curled up under the chair on the other side of the house. He remembered the gaping hole Janice had left in his life and in that moment, he realised how much Stella had come to mean to him, without him even realising.

The murky morning hung heavy in the air painting the streets the colour of wet concrete. Those who ventured out were shrouded in heavy coats, their faces muffled with collars and scarves. The playground stood empty but for a fat pigeon who sat on one of the swings, one foot a deformed stump. As he feared, Frank and Ernie's garage was shut up, but muddy tyre tracks led up to the doors. Exhausted, Norris lay down beside them and put his head on his paws.

So, this new life was to be one of retribution, karma for past sins. Buffeted by the gusts thrown up by passing cars and chilled from the wet ground beneath him, Norris thought back to some of the lives that had come before. He'd grasped each with a selfish enthusiasm, never looking back on past indiscretions, broken promises, irreparable behaviour. Each new existence was an opportunity to explore new pleasures;

see new places. He'd never repeated his choices. Each new life was very different from the last, though he'd found them all equally annoying by the end. By the third reincarnation he'd become braver and more ambitious, and his last life had been no exception. At a mere nineteen years of age, he'd already started planning a new business, one where he alone would get to make the decisions, keeping the best of the rewards, but a world at war and conscription put an end to all that. In Jimmy he'd found a kindred spirit, or so he'd thought. A young man full of life, a risk taker just like Norris, but together their bravado evaporated in the face of fear, a cruel reminder that their destinies were not their own to determine. Now Norris felt manipulated, this new life a mere contrivance to let him look into the mirror and see himself for what he really was, a selfish man. Just as he'd lost his friend, Jimmy, now he'd lost Stella, too and surely, he only had himself to blame.

He'd no idea how much time had passed before he pulled himself up from the ground, his legs stiff beneath him. He slunk back towards fifty-four Grantchester Road and back in through the cat flap. The place felt eerily empty. There was no sign of Mildred or Greg. Two empty mugs sat on the kitchen table amongst a scattering of sugar. Exhausted, Norris dragged himself upstairs and nudged open Stella's bedroom door. He jumped up onto her bed and there he lay until hours later; he heard the front door open and the voices of Mildred and Greg.

"You see, even that solicitor of yours agrees with me. If Jimmy turns King's evidence he could cut years off his sentence."

"But what about Stella?" snapped Mildred. "You know what kidnappers do if you involve the police. I can't lose her, I just can't."

They were the very same words Norris' last wife had uttered as little Janice lay in a fever beneath starched hospital sheets. Hours later, their little daughter took her last breath.

"You've watched too much crappy TV," sneered Greg. "We call the police, just like your solicitor said. He can't charge that much and be wrong."

Norris crept out of Jimmy's room and down the stairs. He didn't want to be there when the police arrived, his only experience with them had left him tarnished. Two lives ago he'd nicked some money as a dare, a measly twenty quid but his parents, ashamed of any child of theirs breaking the law, had marched him down to the police station to confess. The filthy bastards had ripped into him as if he'd tied up a pensioner and ransacked their home. The experience was presumably meant to give him a social conscience but had merely instilled a hatred for the police. No, he wasn't going to hang around, especially as he was sure Mildred was right.

Norris had just nipped past Mildred, who stood in the hall pulling a scarf from around her neck when Greg spotted him.

"Whose idea was that bloody cat?" he said, trying to grab hold of Norris.

"Leave him be," cried Mildred. "Stella loves that cat."

Norris swerved clear of Greg's fingers and dashed across the kitchen and out of the cat flap. Sharp needles of rain pelted his head as he headed through the garden, out of the gate and onto the track. There was only one more place to try, and that was the café.

The streets were busy for late morning and Norris had to weave his way through a forest of legs, narrowly avoiding being kicked by boots or swiped with shopping bags. An old lady bent down to stroke him, but her smile was missing half its teeth, the lines on her face ingrained with grime, her fingernails black with dirt. Norris recoiled, backed up and dashed out into the road, dodging out of the path of a cyclist who shouted expletives into the rain. When Norris reached the café, he jumped up onto one of the outside tables, its plastic cover pooled with water. A fly swam in the ashtray along with the fag butts. The condensation on the window made it hard to make out who sat inside.

There Norris waited until his fur lay soaked against his skin, his bottom in a puddle. Then he heard her, Noreen's voice, but it wasn't coming from inside the café but from behind him.

He went to turn when he felt a hand grab the fold of skin on his neck and he was hoisted into the air.

"Now why would you be here again," said Noreen, holding Norris firmly up in front of her, her fingernails digging into his skin. "You seem to get everywhere, and I don't believe in coincidence." Her teeth were stained with nicotine, and as she spoke the skin around her lips creased, revealing its true colour beneath the layer of foundation which cracked with each word.

Norris thrashed, trying to swipe her with his claws but a sudden spark of an idea made him stop. He let his limbs hang lifeless as she tucked him firmly under her arm and strode away from the café to a small blue car parked a few feet along the street. Noreen opened the car door and shoved him onto the back seat before getting into the driver's seat and slamming the car door behind her.

"Lost your tongue, have you?" she called over her shoulder.

Norris remained silent as she pulled away from the pavement. Noreen had to know something about Stella, maybe she'd even take him to her, after all she had no idea who was really sitting on her back seat, claws latched into the upholstery. As the car sped down the high street, Norris felt once again like a soldier, preparing for a reconnaissance, in the back of an army truck, only this time there was no gun in his hand or knife on his belt and as yet not a single idea of what he could actually do when they arrived at their destination.

Chapter Thirty

Sure enough, Noreen swung the car onto the drive of her bungalow. She parked half on the grass and opened her door. Norris had ample opportunity to escape but instead, he hissed as she swiped him off the back seat and with him firmly wedged under her arm, she opened the door to the bungalow to the excited barks of Spike.

"Get down, you're not having it, not yet anyway." Noreen kicked the terrier with her foot and pushed her way along the hall and through to the lounge, kicking the door shut behind her into the face of Spike. Norris heard Spike's claws attack the closed door as Noreen threw Norris onto the saggy beige sofa, that smelt of fags and sweat. He reared up to his full height, just like a meerkat, but Noreen sat on the armchair opposite and ignored him. She pulled a packet of fags out of her cardigan pocket, plucked out a cigarette and proceeded to light it. She sucked on it, the smoke curling up around her face, her fingers already deeply stained with nicotine, her nails bearing the scratchy remains of nail polish.

"Something about you makes me suspicious," she said, in between drags. "And when I'm suspicious I make damn sure I get to the bottom of it." She leaned nearer to where Norris sat, dropping ash onto a carpet already spotted with burn holes. "You're some kind of celebrity, but more than that, Jimmy took you to that job with him and I intend to find out why."

Two cigarettes later, Noreen opened the door to the lounge, releasing Spike, who catapulted into the room.

Norris had faced the enemy before, men bearing knives, who in those early days made him piss his pants, so an angry terrier was no match for Norris' reaction, which came fast and savage. His claws slashed at one of Spike's ears and nicked his nose. With a pitiful howl, Spike tore out of the room, with his tail between his legs. Norris expected the immediate return of Noreen, but instead he heard a radio playing a pop ballad in another room down the hall and the rumble of a kettle. He leapt off the sofa and scooted out of the sitting room, then silently padded along the corridor and into what looked like Noreen and Frank's bedroom.

He crept around the bed that was draped in a nylon floral bedspread and topped with a cluster of heart-shaped velour cushions their covers snagged in places. A sheepskin rug sat beside the bed. He sniffed it and crawled on his belly to look underneath the bed, but there was nothing there but a balled tissue, a dead spider and one mangy sock. White panelled wardrobes lined one wall of the room and a seventies style dressing table another, its multi-panelled mirror reflecting him three times over as he walked across the bed to reach it. There was a medley of jewellery pots on top, clipped plastic earrings, a hairbrush full of greying hairs and an ashtray overflowing with butts. But there was no clue to suggest Stella had ever been there, not that Norris had expected there to be. He turned and leapt onto the windowsill, nudging past the gaudy poppy curtains which had faded in the sun. The window overlooked the rear garden, almost shin high with grass and thistles. A ramshackle shed propped up a broken fence in one corner, its one window hidden behind metal bars, a chunky padlock on the shed's paint-peeling door. Surely Noreen wasn't stupid enough to stash their jewellery haul in there, but if she had, Norris had no way to get inside, even if he could get out of the bungalow again. He was about to jump back down when he nearly toppled a small photo frame off the windowsill. He steadied it with a paw. It was a picture of two women; one was clearly a much younger Noreen, her hair neatly curled, standing beside a woman who had the same squat nose and wide-set eyes, and a chin that was just a little too pointed. Norris looked closely. Could it be Noreen's sister, Jimmy's wife? The carefully dressed woman held her arm down low but Norris could make out a wedding band on her finger.

So, Jimmy had returned to build a life, with a wife and a daughter, Mildred, but like so many of Norris' marriages, it too had fragmented like a rose battered in a storm. Maybe they weren't so very dissimilar after all. In the regiment they spent so much time together, the others joked they could be brothers. Norris turned his back on the picture and leapt down from the windowsill.

He nipped out of the bedroom and along the hall until he came to the bathroom. The kitchen lay ahead, where he could still hear Noreen clattering about. He was about to dart back down to the sitting room when Spike appeared in the hall, blood drying on his ear.

"You'll pay for that," he yapped.

Norris arched his back and prepared for another attack, but Spike backed away before running towards the sitting room. That just left the bathroom to explore. Inside, the floor tiles were sticky underfoot and although it looked clean enough on first glance there was an underlying smell of pee which made Norris wrinkle his nose. He jumped up to the side of the avocado-coloured bath and tiptoed around the edge. A stained non-slip rubber mat sat in the bottom and a bar of soap lay in a mound of scum beside the tap. He leapt onto the sink and sat in it so he could see what was on the glass shelf above; tooth mugs, a bottle of TCP, a comb and a tub of face cream, its lid not quite screwed on. He was about to turn around to jump back down when Noreen screeched.

"Get out of there!"

She swiped at him. In his surprise, he knocked the shelf above making the tub of face cream tumble into the sink, smacking him on the back. Its lid spun in the shallow of the sink and a large dollop of face cream splattered his feet.

"Now look what you've done."

Noreen thrust her hands towards him. He was expecting her to grab him, but instead she ferreted for something which had fallen out of the tub, and which now clattered in the base of the sink next to his front paws. Quickly she snatched it up, but he'd already seen it, a gold ring with a large red stone. If he hadn't been sitting on the plughole it may have been lost altogether.

Noreen picked him out of the sink and marched him into the sitting room where Spike lay curled up on a dog bed under the window. She dropped Norris onto the sofa and left the two animals together, shutting the door tightly behind her.

So, Noreen had kept a little something from the jewellery haul for herself, probably hidden from Frank who'd be livid if he realised that she had incriminating evidence stashed in their home. It proved her involvement, but Norris hadn't found a single clue as to where Stella might be being held. Spike didn't budge as Norris searched the lounge, but with every step, Norris felt Spike's eyes following him. Never underestimate your enemy, Norris had learned that the hard way. Spike may have retreated for now, but he was sure to be plotting his next move. Every few seconds, Norris looked over to where Spike still lay, watching.

Beside the sofa stood a coffee table upon which lay a bundle of envelopes. A quick forage with his paws showed them to be just utility final demands. Underneath the table lay a copy of the local paper, a half empty packet of cigarettes and a till receipt for milk and bread. A row of cacti and succulents lined the windowsill making it impossible for Norris to walk along it or look outside, so instead he padded over to the corner TV unit and the shelf above it which was filled with a jumble of porcelain figurines, a gold carriage clock and a picture of Noreen and Frank on their wedding day. Time had really not been kind to either of them.

Norris heard the sound of Spike getting up and spun round to find the terrier standing behind him, his feet squarely planted on the carpet, a snarl growing on his face.

"Don't even try it!" hissed Norris. Spike let out a

growl, a deep guttural sound to begin with which grew to a loud bark which sent spittle flying out of his mouth. Norris shot round him and darted behind the sofa, but Spike gave chase. His mouth was about to bite down on Norris' tail when Noreen opened the door to the lounge.

"Get off the poor sod!" she screeched, grabbing hold of Spike's collar and wrenching him up off the floor, until only his back paws touched the carpet. "Hang on a minute, Roger…you stop that, or I'll chain you up outside…it's Spike, I knew Frank should have taken him with him."

The mention of Frank made Norris prick up his ears and extricate himself from where he'd crawled under the sofa.

"Sorry about that…" continued Noreen.

Norris heard the door shut and Spike whining from the hall. With the coast clear, Norris squeezed out from behind the sofa. Noreen sat on the armchair, a phone clamped to her ear, a mug of tea now nestled on the coffee table on top of the bills.

"…it's just that I found that cat lurking outside the café this morning, you call me bonkers if you like but I'll bet it's the same bloody cat that Jimmy had with him in the car, the one the press are falling over themselves to photograph."

There was a pause. Norris couldn't hear the person on the other end of the line so he jumped onto the arm of Noreen's chair and leaned nearer to her.

"…I brought it back here, 'course Spike's taken umbrage to it, he'd rip it apart if I let him and maybe I will."

Norris flinched. As if Noreen had felt it, she looked straight at him and pursed her lips.

"You know, I reckon that cat's more intelligent than Frank, if it weren't just a cat, I could swear he's listening to me right now."

Stop talking about me, yelled Norris in his head, *and let me know who this Roger is.* He inched nearer to Noreen's arm, but the phone was held to the other side of her head and he couldn't make out the individual words of the person on the other end of the line, but Noreen's next words made his heart skip a beat.

"Just keep her quiet, all right. No heavy tactics, just bide your time, Jimmy will come round to our way of thinking soon enough, he's been quiet so far, I reckon he gets what's at stake for him. You should never have brought him into this, that daughter of his is trouble, the meddling cow. And don't tell Frank where you're keeping her neither, just leave him to me."

Roger had to be the third man, and from what Norris was hearing, Noreen was the brains, not Frank, either that or she was keeping things from him, like the ruby ring in the face cream.

"Bring me something of Stella's, something personal, and I'll send it to Mildred, that will put the wind up her."

Noreen burst out laughing.

"Yeah, maybe I should send her a dead cat."

In that second, Norris froze.

Chapter Thirty-One

Norris watched Noreen smoke two more cigarettes. Every window he'd seen was latched shut and there was no other escape route other than the front or back doors, though he'd yet to see the kitchen. He had no intention of ending up as a threat stuffed in a cardboard box for Mildred, so he jumped down from the arm of the chair and headed to the door. Noreen had slumped in the chair, her eyes now closed, a snore rumbling in her throat. Norris wasn't going to find anything else shut in with Noreen, so he clawed the carpet, loudly, so roughly that tufts of pile soon gathered in his claws. He'd almost clawed a hole right down to the underlay when Noreen shook herself awake and hollered across the room.

"No, you don't, you..."

Norris knew only extreme behaviour was likely to get Noreen to open the door, so as soon as her hands grasped his rump he pissed a long stream of urine into the carpet.

"You filthy beast," screeched Noreen, yanking open the sitting room door. Norris was out of her grasp in seconds. He leapt over Spike who lay in wait outside in the hall and streaked down to the kitchen at the end.

"Out of the way," barked Noreen, stumbling over Spike, who whimpered, but Norris was already up on the work surface sniffing at the window above the sink. It was open a couple of inches. Cats could get through the tiniest of gaps, couldn't they, he told himself as he tried unsuccessfully to wedge his head through as

Noreen pulled on his back haunches. She was leaning over the sink, her fingers digging firmly into his rump when the doorbell rang.

"Shit!" she cried, using one hand to pull the window shut and the other to nudge Norris away from it.

"I'll deal with you in a minute."

In her hurry to answer the front door, Noreen failed to shut the kitchen door securely behind her, allowing Norris to ease his way out and back into the hall. He was just calculating how long it would take him to race down the hall and out of the front door as she opened it, when he recognised the figure of the third man nearly filling the entire door frame.

"What are you doing here?" cried Noreen, standing back to let him through. "You can't leave her there alone, Roger, what if she tries to be clever and gets out?"

Roger closed the door behind him, dwarfing Noreen with his bulk. The collar of his overcoat stood up around his thick neck, beads of water glistening on the fabric. His boots left muddy marks on the carpet.

"She ain't going nowhere, so stop fretting. Anyway, I've had quite enough of listening to her complaining."

Norris stopped and stared at Stella's kidnapper. Just as he thought, it was the very same man who'd sat, engine running, outside fifty-four Grantchester Road. Much to Norris' surprise, Noreen's voice softened, and she reached out to place her hand on Roger's arm.

"I'll make us a nice brew," she said, helping Roger off with his coat and hanging it up on the hooks beside the door on top of her own coat, its mauve pockets grubby round the edges and one toggle hanging loose by a thread.

Surely not, thought Norris. *Not behind Frank's back.* Roger spotted Norris in that second and his face creased into a smile.

"That's the bloody cat, it scratched me when I tried to grab it. How did you catch it, it's vicious?"

Noreen giggled. "Sometimes it takes a woman to do things, Roger." She reached up and stroked a finger down his face, then turned and headed back up the hall towards where Norris still sat in the entrance to the kitchen.

Norris couldn't believe his luck when five minutes later, the kettle boiled and the tea made, he sat curled up on the floor looking up at Noreen and Roger who sat drinking tea together at a small table with a blue gingham tablecloth. They were most probably the two brains behind the jewellery heists, and the kidnappers, and they were just four feet away from him but there was sod all he could do to apprehend them. He couldn't exactly ring the police or make a citizen's arrest. Even if he could find a way out, Mildred wasn't going to actually 'listen' to him because he was just a cat.

Out of the corner of his eye he caught a glimpse of Spike who was edging his way nearer to the kitchen.

"How long do you want me to keep the girl?" asked Roger, having drained his tea mug. He unwrapped a toffee from his pocket and began chewing it.

"Those things will rot your teeth," said Noreen.

"Now why would you care about that?" said Roger.

Noreen leaned over the table and tapped him on the nose. "I might like you a little rounded, but I'd rather you keep all your teeth."

Roger took Noreen's hand and squeezed it.

Norris could hear Spike getting nearer behind him and what he needed to hear about was Stella. She must be terrified.

"Just get back to Stella!" he shouted, which of course came out as a wail which made Roger turn round.

"What are you going to do with that cat?"

"I haven't decided yet," said Noreen. "But what I do know is that somehow, it's important to Stella and Jimmy took it with him on the job. Reckon I'll keep it for a while, it might prove useful if Jimmy has any ideas about blabbing."

"Reckon Spike there's going to kill it before you've decided," said Roger.

Hearing his name, Spike stopped his advancement and Norris moved nearer to the table, positioning himself so he could keep an eye on him.

"You wouldn't dare, would you, Spike?"

Spike pricked up his ears and wagged his tail.

"Oh, all right, but you'll have to share today."

Noreen opened a smelly can of dog food and spooned one half into Spike's bowl which sat on a mat halfway along the wall, and one half into a saucer which Noreen set down in front of Norris.

"You might as well eat it," she said, "before Spike does."

The smell of the chunks of unidentified meat coated in greasy gravy made Norris feel sick. He edged away from it as Spike licked his bowl clean, then turned to stare firstly at Norris then at the saucer of food.

"You can have it," meowed Norris.

Spike crept nearer, then nudged the saucer away from

Norris before gulping that food down too.

"Maybe I should take that cat to Stella, it might shut her up for a bit," said Roger, leaning down to stare at Norris, whose heart began to race.

"No way," said Noreen. "Anyway, it would only piss on your aunt's carpet like it did mine and we don't want her knowing you've had anyone there whilst she's been away. And you be careful about any noise, too, you know how nosey her neighbours can be. They think they're posh there, just because that block was opened by the mayor. It's no better than here, at least I don't hang my laundry out of the windows."

"It's not a problem," said Roger. "Her neighbours are expecting me to keep an eye on the place, water her plants, that kind of thing. Don't sweat about it."

A block of flats, a clue at last, now all Norris needed to know was where they bloody well were in a town that size. Stella could be anywhere.

"Just keep her another day or so," said Noreen, "and don't let slip any of this to Frank or Ernie, okay?"

"Sure," said Roger, pushing back his chair to leave.

"You're not thinking of going already, are you?" said Noreen, walking over to his side and taking his hand. "Surely you didn't come over here just for a cup of tea?"

Roger raised an eyebrow and Norris felt sicker than ever.

With a sparkle in her eye and a lightness to her step, Norris watched Noreen lead Roger, the third man, to her bedroom and close the door.

When Norris turned back round, Spike was right in front of him, his mouth open, ready to bite.

Chapter Thirty-Two

Without a second's hesitation, Norris swiped Spike across the nose with a viciousness that drew blood, then he sprang at the terrier with a surge of adrenalin which pumped through his veins. With fluffs of fur flying and a tangle of limbs, the pair wrestled on the floor outside Noreen's bedroom door, which remained firmly shut.

Norris had learnt quickly never to give the enemy the chance to make the first move. Now he smelt Spike's breath in his nostrils and his fear with it. Pinned to the floor, with Norris latched firmly on his back, Spike let out a howl.

"You bastard!"

Norris dug in his claws.

"I'll soon be gone, but until I do, keep your filthy mouth to yourself."

Spike whimpered as blood oozed from the scratches into his fur. Norris clambered down and licked the blood from his paws, watching out of the corner of his eye, as Spike slunk into the sitting room. From inside Noreen's bedroom came the creaking of the bed. Norris headed off to the kitchen to explore.

He jumped up onto the work surface; storage jars labelled tea, coffee and sugar lined the Formica top. He stepped over the kettle flex and spied an open packet of biscuits. He was ravenous. Patting it over with his paw, he managed to roll it towards him, releasing a tumble of digestive biscuits. He ate them all, his front now littered with crumbs and his whiskers too. He shook his head and licked his fur. He really couldn't get used to fur sticking to his tongue and slipping down his throat. He wondered how long it would be before a knot of hair lodged in his stomach and he had to vomit it up like a hairy turd onto the floor. He leapt from one countertop to the other and onto the draining board. A pool of water sat in the bottom of the washing bowl, and he lapped some if it up, though it took a ridiculously long time to quench his thirst. When he'd finished, he stared out of the window, at the straggle of thistles and clumps of nettles. It was just as soulless as Jimmy's garden.

His thoughts went to Stella, trapped alone somewhere in a flat, wondering what might happen to her. Oh Jimmy, how could you let this happen to Stella, of all people. How could you be so stupid? Surely the police would be out searching for her, Greg would have seen to that. Jimmy could have spared everyone if he'd done the decent thing, the right thing, but who was Norris to condemn him? He'd done a despicable, cowardly thing and now maybe he'd lose Stella, just like he lost Janice.

His thoughts were broken by voices coming from Noreen's bedroom and the sound of feet heading to the door. He jumped down from the sink and ran along the hall to the front door. When that door opened, and surely it would, he needed to be ready. The shabby hall table offered no hiding place so, as Noreen's bedroom door creaked open, Norris squeezed himself behind a heap of shoes, boots and wellies, tucking his tail in tightly around him and there he waited.

"Now shove off," giggled Noreen.

"Right," said Roger. "I'll get the package delivered, but I need her out of that flat tomorrow, one way or another."

"Just you make sure that nephew of yours doesn't get caught, he's got form, and there'll be too many questions."

Their voices were almost above where Norris was hiding. He may only have a second. He popped his head out to see Noreen reach for the front door and turn the handle. He unfurled his tail and braced himself. As Noreen opened the door, letting in a gust of wind, Norris streaked through the gap like a greyhound off the starting line and he was gone before Noreen could even utter a word.

He ran and he kept running, down the path and onto the road, hurtling down the pavement. If they came after him, they were far too slow to catch him. He didn't stop at the curb, but darted out between the traffic, narrowly missing the wheels of a transit van and making a motorcycle swerve to avoid him. Grantchester Road lay ahead. His heart pounded between his ribs, an ache running down all four legs. He was just two houses away when the piercing shriek of a cat fight made him slow his pace. In the front garden of number fifty-two, under a hydrangea bush, he caught sight of Boris being mauled by a bruiser of a black cat, even burlier than Boris. Now, Norris had grown to loathe the sight of Boris, but he couldn't help peer over the low wall at them. Maybe he wanted to see Boris on the receiving end for a change but what he saw was pure terror in Boris's green eyes, and complete surrender in his flattened ears, and though

Norris wanted to, he just couldn't walk on by. He hated a bully, any bully, and though he may have been half the size of the black cat, he was a trained killer, and he was sure that had to give him some kind of advantage.

Norris leapt over the wall and launched himself on top of the black cat, ripping into his shoulder with his claws. He wasn't sure who was more surprised, the black cat, who howled in pain, or Boris who stared up at him before taking advantage of the distraction he needed and squirming out from beneath them both and delivering a cruel blow to the head of his attacker, swiftly followed by another. Outnumbered and outwitted, the black cat shrank down in the grass, a deep growl rumbling in its throat. With a screaming hiss, it turned and fled back through the garden and down a side alley beside the house.

Boris turned to Norris and if a cat could smile, Norris was sure he did.

"Bloody hell, where did you come from, not that I needed any help."

"Yeah right," meowed Norris. "He was pulverising you and you know it."

"A nasty little bastard, that one," meowed Boris. "He must have been a psycho in a previous life."

"That's something coming from you," meowed Norris, though he was wondering something which niggled like a thorn in the pad of his foot.

"Yeah well, when you've had the crap beaten out of you in more than one life, it changes you, don't it?"

"Did you say what I think you just said?" meowed Norris.

"Have you lost your human brains? Come on, you

should have figured it out by now! We cats are all here for a reason, none of us chose to be trapped inside these pathetic bodies, forced to lick our own arses. We're all here because we made some pretty crap choices in our human lives, couldn't even get those right with eight chances, so here we are to work something out, I guess."

Norris' heart thundered. So, this wasn't some sick game just for him, but for all losers who blew it big time in the human world.

"So, what did you do wrong?" meowed Norris.

"Hurt the ones who should have meant the most, killed someone who didn't deserve to die, you name it. And you?"

Norris couldn't believe what he was hearing. Were all cats screwed up humans, or those with demons to chase? "I betrayed a friend," meowed Norris.

"Is that all? You did better than many of us." Boris turned to go. "I won't forget today, just saying," And then he slipped through the hedge and was gone.

Norris sat on the wall and let the revelation sink in. How stupid of him to think he had somehow been singled out and then, the more he thought about it, how obvious it should have been that cats were for too intelligent to have just been animals like any other. And Norris was still sitting on that wall when the light took on the warm tinge of evening and he suddenly remembered Stella.

Shaking himself, he jumped down from the wall and trotted along past number fifty-four, where the curtains were still closed, down the track, up and over the wall and across the garden to the cat flap. He arrived back in the kitchen to hear Mildred crying softly across the hall. There had been no police car out in the road and no sign of police in the house. Instead, Mildred sat in Jimmy's chair, sobbing, holding in her lap a small bear which Norris recognised as having sat on Stella's bed. So, the package had been delivered already and Norris had missed it. Greg stood beside Mildred with his arms cradling her shoulders, shushing her gently and Mildred had one of his hands clasped within her own.

"Okay, I agree, no police, not yet," said Greg softly. "But you have to get word to Jimmy, he needs to know what he's done."

Oh, he'll know already, thought Norris. Noreen will have made sure of that, just as she'd made sure he got a few fists in the face inside too. Noreen's message would be very clear indeed.

Chapter Thirty-Three

The hours ticked over and all Norris could do was pace. How many blocks of flats could there possibly be? But without a name or street, what use was a street map even if Jimmy had one somewhere. Mildred had spent an hour on the telephone with Greg never far from her side, Stella's bear held tightly in her hand. The friction that had crackled so fiercely in the air when Greg first arrived, had morphed into a mutually supportive tolerance. It was still hard to picture the two of them romantically entwined, but they were able to pull together in a common cause, something Norris himself was unable to do when his beloved Janice lay dying in hospital, and he couldn't even find enough emotional connection with his last wife to hold her hand as she sat crying silently next to his daughter's bedside. Maybe Boris had been right, he had a lot to learn.

Norris gleaned little from the telephone conversations that he'd heard other than Mildred was desperately seeking permission to visit Jimmy, and it would seem unlikely to meet with success, so Norris decided to stop waiting for his supper, which was unlikely to arrive anytime soon, and he pushed his way out of the cat flap and out into the darkening evening, made darker still by heavy cloud which shrouded the moon. There was no sign of Boris as he made his way along the track and back to the front of the house on Grantchester Road. Despite the growing gloom, the road was busy with traffic, the cars' headlights illuminating the path as Norris trotted along it. Stella was facing a second night away from home and still no-one was looking for her, and Norris had no idea where to start. But, unlike when Janice had slipped away in the small hours, Norris wouldn't just pace helplessly up and down the corridor outside her room, he was going to do everything, indeed, anything he had to, to save Stella. He walked half the length of Grantchester Road, away from the town when he noticed a lady standing by a bus stop, the tip of her lit cigarette glowing, a big yellow scarf muffled around her shoulders. She put out her hand and a large double decker bus pulled into the kerb, its indicators flashing, its doors swinging open, flooding the pavement with light. On an impulse, Norris nipped around her legs and jumped aboard. The driver, who surely hadn't seen him, closed the doors and the bus jolted forward and joined the traffic, sending Norris skidding down the aisle until he managed to wedge himself by one of the seats. Now, as the bus picked up speed, he jumped up onto an empty seat and sat up straight, looking out of the window. The streets were well lit with streetlights and soon Norris was further than the lock ups and heading deep into the residential areas of town.

His fellow passengers whispered and nudged one another, they'd probably never seen a cat on a bus before. One old lady changed seats to sit beside him and stroked him affectionately which he bore with good grace but without turning round because he was focused on the streets, looking for any sign of blocks of flats. His military training meant he had a great sense of direction and a good memory for routes. Every street was lodged in his memory as the bus headed into a sprawling housing estate.

"Now, where do you think you're going?" said the woman, still stroking his head. "Maybe I should take you home. You don't have a collar do you, or maybe you're just lost."

A young lad leaned over the old lady and snapped a camera, the flash made Norris jump.

"They're never going to believe this at school," laughed the boy.

For a brief second, Norris looked away from the window but then when he looked back, he saw them; a row of tower blocks, seventies concrete flats, with balconies, some filled with plants, others with bicycles and more than one with abandoned washing which flapped in the wind.

Norris leapt over the lap of the old lady, and ran down the aisle wailing loudly so the driver couldn't fail to hear him. A man with a huge green umbrella already stood by the door as the bus pulled into the side of the road and Norris nipped out before him and onto the pavement. The bus closed its doors and pulled away but not before Norris clocked its service number on the back, the number 128. The man opened his umbrella as the first spits of rain fell and left Norris standing at the bus stop. He noted the number of the stop, and the bus timetable that stood in the bus shelter, one side of glass smashed so cubes of shattered glass littered the floor, which itself was strewn with beer cans, fag butts and a broken umbrella. In the street behind him, the tower blocks loomed above him, but there were at least four of them and they all looked the same. Maybe Stella was even now sitting in one of them, or maybe Roger had moved her already. Norris stood looking up at the buildings which dwarfed him, a tiny ginger cat in a concrete maze and suddenly he felt so very small and so very inadequate.

For what seemed like minutes, he dithered. He felt like a young recruit again, greener than the first pea shoots of the season and for a brief moment his insides wobbled, then he reminded himself he'd not only survived that first month of service, but had killed not once, but twice. He pulled himself up to his full height, set one foot steadfastly in front of another and set off towards the first block of flats in Dewsbury Close.

He walked all around the first block, its entrance hall swamped in shadow, a gang of youths huddled just at the bottom of the steps passing a beer can between them, laughing. One of them spotted Norris and jeering, he lobbed the can towards him. It whizzed just past Norris' head, spraying him with sticky beer. Instinct told him to run, and his instinct was rarely wrong. The path led him to the second block, as characterless as the last. He looked up at the endless sea of windows. Could Stella be sitting behind one of them, looking down to the street below to the speck of orange in the shadows which was Norris, as likely to find her and rescue her as the postman was to climb all those stairs without breaking into a sweat.

Norris slumped down to the pavement beside the entrance door. His ears sagged and there he sat until his fur was saturated with rain and drips fell from his nose to join the ever-increasing puddle beneath him. He may even have nodded off until the sudden smell of a rat scurrying past him woke him. What use was he to Stella sitting here? He shook himself, splattering raindrops against the already wet concrete wall and trudged towards the next block of flats, his speed hampered by the now constant slant of rain which drove water into every recess of his body and under every layer of fur. Stella could be anywhere, he hadn't even started looking and without a strategy of some kind, he may as well catch the next bus back to Grantchester Road or walk out under the next bus come to that, for all the good he was doing. He waded through a pattern of puddles, when a toffee wrapper seemed to swim towards him like a boat at sea. His tail shot out straight in recognition. Roger! Roger and his dropped toffee wrappers, like a trail of breadcrumbs for the children in Hansel and Gretel. Norris set off along the path, splashing through the puddles to the entrance hall of the third block of flats. The door was wedged open and a steep flight of stairs led up to the block above him. He bounded up the first flight with renewed energy and sure enough, there sat another wrapper. Norris sniffed it. It still reeked of rum, rum and raisin toffees. What Norris wouldn't give for a tot of rum right then to ward off the cold which made his damp legs shiver, but he'd settle for another toffee wrapper on the next flight of stairs. This had to be the block where Roger's aunt had her flat, where Stella was waiting, and Roger was watching.

Two more flights of stairs and there were no more wrappers, so he headed back down to the last wrapper he'd found and bounded along the corridor in front of the row of doors dodging bags of rubbish, bicycles and even a rusted pram and smelly old mattress until two more wrappers later something made him stop. Unlike some of the other flats this one's outside space was spotless and well cared for, the door flanked with flowerpots. He looked up at the window beside the blue painted door, number seventy-two, and inside the windowsill was crammed full of plants. What had Roger said to Mildred? His aunt wanted him to water her plants. This could be it; it had to be.

Norris jumped up to the window ledge and balanced precariously, it was so narrow, his tail was all a-tremble. Between the jungle of leaves he could just see a light in a hallway beyond. Willing himself to stay balanced, Norris waited, for so long that every muscle ached in the effort to stay where he was until finally, as he thought he'd lose all feeling in his feet and would plummet to the concrete below, he saw a figure in the hallway, a glimpse, just a glimpse but it was definitely Roger. If Roger was here, so too must be Stella.

Chapter Thirty-Four

In Norris' excitement, he wobbled like a trainee tightrope walker on a wire, lost his footing and tumbled to the ground below, landing bottom first in a flowerpot, the stem of the hydrangea plant poking him where it hurt. In an ungainly manoeuvre, he wriggled himself free and toppled onto the concrete below. Close inspection of the front door revealed no way in for a cat and the window he'd been looking in at was the only window of the flat on that side of the building. Not for the first time, he wished he had an opposable thumb and a house breaking kit. As it was, all he could do was wait for Roger to leave and after so much waiting he really didn't have the patience for it. He began pacing, hoping inspiration would dawn on him but nothing did, except how bloody inconvenient it was to be a cat. Give him a knife, a piece of wire or even a hairpin and as a human he'd have been in in under five minutes. He was ashamed to remember, he'd done it before.

So, what were cats good at? Like many before him, he'd often wondered why people had cats at all, they just scratched the furniture and shat in your flower beds. Those he'd known in his lives had been aloof and indeed treated humans as inferior, which of course, now made perfect sense because with eight lives already behind them, cats surely didn't need humans at all except to feed them and give them a warm place to sleep. But he too had watched the antics of cats; they were great hunters, could even be ninja's if they put their minds to it and could make one hell of a noise with their caterwauling, and this gave Norris an idea. It wasn't much of one, but it might just work. If he could make enough of a noise, maybe Roger would open that door, it need only be a fraction and only for a second but then Norris would be in.

Norris scouted out the immediate vicinity to see what could help him, and then he set to work. First, he threw himself at the offending flowerpot which had broken his fall earlier and sent it crashing over, soon followed by its partner which had sat the other side of the door. He filled his lungs and launched into a manic caterwauling session, reaching higher notes than he even imagined his vocal cords could reach whilst pushing the rusted pram from next door against the wall, sending two bicycles clattering as he rammed into them. But did the front door or the window open? Like hell it did! In his frustration, Norris shrieked some more. Roger may have chosen not to notice but unfortunately for Norris, someone else had. And that someone now stood at the end of the corridor watching Norris make a spectacle of himself and he wasn't alone. Clearly alerted to the possibility of some Wednesday evening sport, a spotty teenager and his two friends now advanced on Norris, loudly egging each other on.

"Look at that bloody cat, must have something wrong with its brain to kick off like that," laughed one lad, pointing at Norris, who had frozen on the spot like a rabbit in headlights because the two friends weren't next to the boy who now ran towards Norris, but were advancing behind him.

"I saw it first," hollered the boy, "so I get first kick."

Before Norris could find an escape route, he felt

himself being hoisted up by the scruff of his neck.

"Maybe it's got rabies," laughed the boy who swung Norris in front of him like a pendulum.

"Give it to me," came a girl's voice.

"Take your turn," snarled the boy, "I got here first."

Awful images of louts torturing kittens came to mind and Norris waggled his legs furiously trying to free himself but when the boy just held on firmer, Norris knew innovative action might be all that could save him. He released a stream of urine in a gush which splashed onto the boy's trainers.

"You filthy beast," howled the boy, tossing Norris into the air. "Mum will kill me, she only got these yesterday."

Norris took his chance and tried to dart between the legs of the other boy who barred his way along the corridor.

"No, you don't," he laughed, grabbing hold of Norris around the middle.

With a twist of his head, Norris sunk his teeth into the nearest piece of flesh which proved to be the boy's finger.

The boy screeched. "What if it's really got rabies?"

"Then you're dead," laughed the girl, grabbing hold of Norris' tail and giving it such a yank that Norris thought she'd pull it right off.

Every hair on Norris' body sprung on end and he spun round lashing out at anything and everything that came near him. And despite his wails and incessant hissing and the cries of the ever more excited youths that tried to catch him, still the front door to the flat never opened. But Norris had seen places like this before, estates where doors remained tightly shut, not out of indifference but out of fear and it was just his luck he'd walked into just such a neighbourhood on an impossible mission. In his desperation to escape, Norris looked at the only direction which offered a way out, right over the concrete balcony wall to the three story drop below.

He'd learnt many things very quickly in the war, and one of those was to take the almost least survivable option available if it were the only option that presented itself in the second or two you had to think. When it was the enemy or you, you took the chance which was offered. He'd seen more times than he wanted to remember, young men cut down because they paused too long or were stupid enough to think combat rewarded the hero. Norris had unwittingly grown to love Stella dearly, but no matter how much he needed to get into that flat, he wasn't going to hang around a second longer because a dead cat was never going to save anyone. In the next half second, Norris faced the balcony and the night beyond and he launched himself up and over it, free falling to the concrete path below.

As he fell and the wet wind rushed past him, he prayed that cats really were natural fallers and that no matter the height, they always landed on their feet. But as the ground shot up towards him, he realised maybe that meant the height of a garden wall not three floors up a block of flats. Oh shit!

As the ground met his feet, one of his paws buckled sending a searing pain through his whole body but he was alive, and from what he could feel, in one piece and he was well away from the kids who would have killed him if he'd stayed. That had to be a result but as Norris looked around him, he also realised Stella was still locked in a flat and he was far from Grantchester Road in the rain without any kind of plan at all.

Chapter Thirty-Five

With a reluctance which hurt almost as much as his foot, Norris limped away from the blocks of flats and back to the bus stop on the other side of the road. Two buses drove straight past him and it wasn't until a young girl flagged down the next bus that Norris could jump aboard. This bus was packed and with no seats free, he crouched in the luggage rack at the front on top of a folded pushchair. Worried the bus might not stop at Grantchester Road, Norris got off earlier when the young mother retrieved the pushchair and disembarked. So it was that by the time Norris made it back to Grantchester Road, he was more than limping, he was dragging his bruised paw along, making his gait sway. He'd got to outside fifty-two Grantchester Road when he saw Boris nipping out of the front door and he was heading straight for him.

"I'm not the only one with battle wounds then," laughed Boris. A smelly ointment was slicked across his ear and down his shoulder making it look like he'd applied a generous slap of Brylcreem.

Norris sat down, relieved to take the weight off his legs. When he'd caught his breath, he meowed, "I jumped from a block of flats."

"Bloody hell," replied Boris. "Cats can't do that!"

"Who says so?" meowed Norris. "In this screwed up life, I reckon we do what we have to."

Boris joined Norris on the pavement. "Guess you're not wrong there. Some days I feel like I've been dumped in a play, and no-one's bothered to tell me what the crap it's about. What made you do it?"

Of course, Norris had no idea where to begin with that story so instead he nodded over to the house behind them. "You live here, just next door to mine?"

"I've been here a while. Well, since Lucinda, her indoors, pulled me out of a cardboard box from a ditch at the side of the road. Must have been five, six years ago now."

Norris thought of the day Stella picked him out of the cat rescue place and brought him back to Jimmy's house, and the realisation hit him that if this really was some kind of sick game, then it was no coincidence that he was chosen by Stella. He'd never considered himself a believer in conspiracy theories before, and he was no great lover of fiction either, but if the reality of what seemed to be the case was true, hell, no-one could have made that shit up. It was more than sick, it was perverted, the worst kind of torture any human could be put through. If this all really was some kind of mind game, it was definitely messing with his head.

"I was a filthy little scrag of a kitten then," meowed Boris, "but I recognised Lucinda from the pictures in the paper and when she put me in the bath to wash me, well, I thought she was going to drown me, and I'd have deserved it, of course."

"Why, why would she do that if she'd rescued you?" meowed Norris.

"Weren't you listening before, or do you really not get it? Of course, she'd drown me if she knew who I really was, I'd killed her mother!"

It was the last thing Norris had expected Boris to say and for a second, he couldn't even search for the words to utter next.

"Of course, I didn't mean to kill her, I was drunk, too absorbed in stuff in my head when she stepped out in front of my car, but I didn't stop, I never bothered to go back and somehow, they never found me, well, not until this life. Looks like everything catches up with you in the end."

Norris felt like he was in a confessional, and maybe he should have tried that in his last life, but religion had meant nothing to him, he was far too cocky believing he was invincible. "I left a friend to the Nazis, saved myself instead."

"Ah," meowed Boris. "But how does that find you jumping off a tower block? You're no soldier now."

"I'm trying, or I was, to save someone, someone who's innocent in all this, but as a cat, I might as well be dead for all the use I am to her."

"You give up too easily," meowed Boris. "If I can help, I owe you."

With that, Boris wandered off, leaving Norris sitting on the pavement.

With a will he almost didn't have, Norris made it back to the cat flap at fifty-four Grantchester Road and almost fell inside. Mildred was washing up at the sink, when she heard him, and she turned round to where he'd crawled onto the kitchen lino.

"Where have you been?" she cried, pulling off her Marigolds and scooping him up. "Greg, come here, looks like Stella's cat's been hit by a car, his paw is all floppy, maybe it's broken."

Greg sauntered into the kitchen and peered at Norris. "Nah, probably just been fighting. Since when were you all soppy about a cat?"

"Stella loves this cat, sometimes I think she loves it more than me, that's why and when…when we get her back, he needs to be here for her, waiting for her…she…"

"We'll get her back, you'll see."

Mildred nodded and let Greg pull her into a hug, which squished Norris, but he was too weak to even meow.

"We'll get that note that the kidnapper left with Stella's bear to Jimmy tomorrow, your solicitor promised she would."

Norris pricked up his ears. Note? Note? This was it, what he needed to do, and he needed to do it now. He wriggled so much that Mildred popped him down on the floor by the bowl Greg had filled with chunks of tuna in oil.

"See, he's hungry already."

And Norris, absolutely famished, wolfed down the lot as the ideas swam around inside his head. How can a cat write a note? Think! Think! Think! Cats can't write, he'd tried that. They can't cut and paste letters from the newspaper either, no thumbs but, just maybe they could type. Now where had he seen a typewriter? If monkeys could type, and hadn't it been suggested that if a monkey was given long enough it could randomly type the works of Shakespeare, so could a cat. Norris needed to do it and quickly…just a short note, a few words would do.

Despite the throbbing of his paw, Norris made it up the stairs. He'd seen a typewriter, but where? It wasn't in Stella and Mildred's room. He padded down the corridor to Jimmy's room, the door was still open. Mildred had clearly been tidying since his arrest, for the bureau was closed again. Norris had almost given up hope of finding it, when he remembered it was under Jimmy's bed, he'd seen it there when he'd been sitting on the rug watching Jimmy's room being searched. Norris crawled on his belly to look and yes, there it was, with one sheet of paper still clipped into place with half a typed letter on it.

Norris squeezed his way under the bed and putting the top of his head on the back of the metal typewriter he shunted it forwards, a few millimetres at a time until it sat on the floor in front of the bed. He was surprised to see the letter in the typewriter was addressed to Mildred.

"Dear Mildred,
If you're reading this, it's because the police have traced me. Don't be angry, I only did what I had to do, or the bank would have taken away this house. This is your home and always will be..."

That was it, no other explanation and it was unsigned which made Norris think Jimmy hadn't finished typing it; when he left that morning for the robbery, he clearly thought he was coming home again that day. Oh, how wrong he'd been.

Norris heard Greg and Mildred's voices drifting up the stairs. He had no idea how long he had before they might come upstairs and hear him. He scanned the typewriter's keys and tried to familiarise himself with the layout and functions. With an effort he managed to leave a few spaces after Jimmy's words and then he hit those keys as hard as he could to move the little hammers up to the ribbon. It took far more strength than he ever imagined but slowly and very loudly, the words began to appear on the paper.

"...let Stella go. I know what you did."

When Norris had finished, his paws throbbed. He pulled the paper out of the typewriter with his mouth and pushed the typewriter painfully back under the bed. Then he stood on the paper and carefully with his mouth tore off the top section with Jimmy's letter and this he shoved with his paw back under the bed. Now the note for Roger lay on the rug in front of him. He had no idea how late the buses ran but he had to somehow get that note to the attention of Roger and with regret he knew that meant pulling in the favour from Boris, who owed him.

Chapter Thirty-Six

With his rolled up note in his mouth, Norris hobbled down the stairs and out of the cat flap. It was so much harder to balance, somehow, with something clinched between his teeth and he wobbled on the top of the garden wall, just managing to jump down to the track below before he fell. Now to find Boris before the piece of paper in his mouth became mush, but it seemed Boris hadn't gone far. The tortoiseshell cat sat washing beside an overflowing dustbin on the track and heard Norris' approach.

"What you got there?" he meowed.

Norris really didn't want to go into details but he dropped the note so he could reply.

"I need to ask you for that favour, I can't really explain but I need your help back at that block of flats."

"Sounds like an adventure," meowed Boris.

"Really it's a rescue mission," meowed Norris, "and it means catching a bus, if they're still running this late."

"A bus? No way, no self-respecting cat gets on one of those."

"It's too far to walk, and…"

"You haven't been a cat long, have you?" meowed Boris. "Us cats roam vast distances, we know every cut through, every alleyway, just tell me roughly where you want to get to and I'll navigate the way, trust me, I never get lost."

Norris did his best to explain, then with difficulty, he re-rolled up the note, the back of which was now covered in mud, and he followed Boris, who set a steady pace along Grantchester Road and then down an alleyway which cut across the back of an estate. With no streetlamps anywhere in sight, Norris was grateful for the eyesight he really could have used back in France. Together they weaved their way across town, nipping through gardens and skirting round garages. When at last they were back near the main road that the bus had driven along and the blocks of flats lit the skyline with their windows burning bright, Norris' foot was so tender he'd developed a pronounced limp that made him sway as he walked, and he wondered how would ever manage the journey back.

Boris stopped and looked up at the blocks of flats. "So, why did you need my help?" he meowed, but Norris carried on walking, leading the way this time until he reached the block of flats where he hoped he'd still find Stella. Boris followed.

Anyone who saw them may well have wondered why a small ginger cat was climbing the stairs of a block of flats carrying a tube of paper in its mouth, followed by a large tortoiseshell cat. Luckily, there was no sign of the youths of earlier and after carefully counting the flights of stairs to make sure he reached the right landing, Norris led the way along the concrete balcony until he reached number seventy-two, the flat of Roger's aunt. The hydrangeas lay in a mound of broken pot and earth and the rusted pram still blocked the doorway, so it would seem Roger was still inside. Norris dropped the note onto the concrete floor and gestured with his head to the letterbox.

"I need to get this note through there," he meowed. "Then we need to knock on that door in the hope the man inside comes to see who's there."

"Easy," meowed Boris. He pushed the pram away with his head so that it trundled along the balcony as if it were being pushed by a ghost, then he positioned himself directly below the letterbox. "Climb up onto my back, you should be able to reach. Careful, those letterboxes can spring back all of a sudden. Watch your nose, I used to be a postman, some can be vicious buggers, one nearly took my fingers off."

It was just as well Boris was so stocky because on his first attempt, Norris misjudged his jump and tumbled over Boris's head and back to the ground. On a second attempt, he landed squarely between Boris's shoulders. It was still quite a stretch to reach the letterbox, and it took an age to negotiate pushing it open with his nose and trying to stuff the note through cleanly without being snared by the jaws of the letterbox, but finally he saw it flutter to the doormat below. Now with every ounce of stamina he had left, he snapped that letterbox flap open and shut until at last he heard footsteps inside heading their way.

"He's coming," meowed Norris, leaping down from Boris's back. He winced as his paw bent back over, making his eyes smart with the pain.

"What you going to do if he opens the door?" meowed Boris.

"Get inside, of course," meowed Norris. "You create a diversion, take a chunk out of his leg if you have to."

"I hear you," meowed Boris.

Norris hadn't really thought beyond delivering the note and as the door began to open, the outline of Roger behind the glass, Norris was still trying to compute his next move but as it turned out he'd underestimated Stella.

The door opened to reveal Roger, clutching Norris' note, open in his hand. Boris was braced to attack, and Norris had already positioned himself to dart between Roger's legs when someone came up behind Roger and walloped him on the head with a saucepan, making Roger stagger wildly in the doorway, seconds later tumbling to the ground with an almighty crash. Stella triumphantly waved the saucepan, pushed past him and out onto the balcony. There she froze, for by her ankles stood Norris and beside him a large tortoiseshell cat.

"Norris, is that you?" She stepped over the body of Roger, who moaned softly on the ground, and bent down to where Norris stood.

"It is you, isn't it? How did you know where to find me?"

"I didn't see that coming," laughed Boris.

"Who's your friend?" said Stella, scooping Norris up off the ground and giving him a hug. "If it wasn't such a ridiculous idea, I'd say you weren't a cat at all," she said, squeezing him. "But of course you are, just look at you." She lifted him up to her face. "Hey, what happened to your paw?"

Norris' injured paw hung limply, and he let out an involuntary meow when she tried to touch it. "Let's get you home, Norris, before he comes round."

Norris looked down at Boris, who sniffed around Roger, unconscious now on the ground.

"Looks like you've got this covered," he meowed. "I'll leave you to it." He flicked his tail and padded off along the balcony, back towards the staircase.

It was then that Stella noticed the note. She kicked it out of Roger's hand and peered down to read it. "Is this something to do with you?" she said, looking again at Norris. "No, that's impossible...but..."

Norris meowed, "Yes!" But of course, Stella couldn't understand his meows but for that brief moment he didn't care, he had Stella back, that was all that mattered. She carried him, cradling him close to her as she ran along the balcony and down the stairs until she reached the main entrance below. Outside the wind blew her hair and Norris' face. He wondered if she knew her way home but then reminded himself, she had proven far more resourceful than he'd given her credit for. On the long walk back, lulled by the rhythm of her walk and utterly exhausted, Norris must have nodded off for when he opened his eyes again, they were walking down the garden path to fifty-four Grantchester Road. Stella pressed the front doorbell and waited. A few seconds later Mildred flung open the front door and burst into tears.

"What the..." gasped Greg, who came up behind her. "How the..."

Mildred bundled Stella and Norris into her arms. "I thought I'd never see you again," sobbed Mildred.

Greg stared at Norris. "What is it with that cat...it gets everywhere."

Stella pulled herself free and headed inside the house, carrying Norris. "I've been trying to tell you Mum, Norris is no ordinary cat. He found me, if it wasn't for him, I'd still be locked in that flat."

"Flat, what flat?" cried Mildred. "Who did this, Stella?"

"I've no idea who he was, Mum," said Stella, "but I've seen him before, sitting in a car outside this house, watching us."

Norris of course, knew exactly who Roger was and what he was, but he was still no nearer to being able to tell Stella that.

Chapter Thirty-Seven

The debate about whether to call the police ran well into the night but after two rounds of tea, and a pile of toast and butter, Stella took herself off to bed leaving Mildred and Greg in the sitting room.

"I'll be up soon," Mildred called up the stairs.

"I'm all right, Mum," called back Stella, "I'm not a kid anymore."

Norris kept very close and as Stella pulled the duvet up to her neck, the teddy bear tucked near her chin, he curled up on top of her legs. She was a lot tougher and more resourceful than Mildred could ever guess. Roger would have a stinking headache at best, but then, it was probably just the adrenaline talking, rather than masterful planning on Stella's part. Norris knew when the risks were high and danger was your enemy, a primal force took over, giving even the young or weak a terrifying burst of resilience, which had seen soldiers carry wounded comrades under enemy fire and trapped women and children crawl out of bullet riddled rubble. But what did Norris do? Fight or flight. He ran like a coward. Not Stella, she had more gumption that he'd ever had, and Jimmy should be very proud indeed, though Norris doubted Stella would ever tell and Roger would never admit a young girl had laid him out cold, though Norris would have loved to know how Roger would explain Stella's escape to Noreen.

When Mildred had finally come to bed and her snores were all Norris could hear, he crept down from Stella's bed and into Jimmy's room. Again, he pushed the typewriter out from under the bed but realised too late that it no longer held any paper. So much for typing Stella a note. With a mighty shove with his shoulder, the typewriter was back under the bed and Norris sagged onto the rug, beneath which, still hidden beneath the loose floorboard, lay the roll of money and box of bullets. The hours ticked over until a shaft of early light filtered through Jimmy's curtains. It was dawn but all in the house slept, oblivious to the chorus of birds outside and the dilemma that had kept Norris awake all night. Stella was home, safe for now, but Jimmy lay in a prison cell awaiting trial and still the real criminals would be planning their next move. Stella could identify Roger in a line-up, anyway, but somehow Norris doubted the flat where he'd kept her would link Roger to any other crime and he'd be long gone once Noreen realised how much of a liability he really was. It wasn't love he'd seen in Noreen's bungalow, but the thrill of Noreen having her own bit of excitement in a life as dull as her own choice in home furnishings. No, she wouldn't think twice about ridding herself of Roger. But then, Norris remembered the ruby ring, hidden in the tub of face cream, the one thing which could find Noreen, Frank and Ernie in a cell just like Jimmy's. That's when Norris' plan began to come together.

Back in Mildred and Stella's bedroom, Norris rooted amongst Mildred's things on the shelf near her bed. She lay, mouth open, hair swept across her eyes, one arm hanging over the side of the bed and one foot sticking out of the duvet. Stella was curled up on her side facing away from him. He stuck his nose into an open make-up bag, sniffed around for a few seconds, then clamped his teeth around a lipstick. Soundlessly he carried it into the bathroom and jumped up onto the sink beneath the mirror. It took many attempts, chasing the lipstick around the bowl of the sink to capture it under his paw and pull off the lid with his teeth. The bright crimson lipstick left squiggles on the sink before he captured it again, the plastic end in his mouth. He raised himself up on his hind legs like a meerkat, then leaned towards the mirror. Slowly and meticulously, he drew the letters onto the glass, taking care not to smear them. Brevity was essential, he just hoped he'd written enough. He spat the stump of the lipstick into the sink then jumped back down and positioned himself just inside the door to Jimmy's room. That's where he waited more than two hours before he heard Mildred shouting.

"Greg! Get up here now. Stella!"

Norris, stiff with fatigue, headed onto the landing to see Mildred, Greg and Stella standing in the bathroom. Before them, scrawled on the mirror were the words,

"Noreen and Frank are the robbers"

It wasn't the best English Norris could have written, but he was pleased with himself that it conveyed all it needed to, for now.

"Stella, was that you?" cried Mildred, snatching up what was left of her lipstick from the sink."

"No, Mum...why would I..."

"I told you we should have left here last night," butted in Greg, pushing in front of Mildred. "Someone's been here, whilst we slept…they could have done anything…"

"Are you sure?" said Mildred. "Check the doors and windows and…we really should have called the police; you were right but…"

"Wait!" cried Stella. "Just wait a minute. The man who took me, he'd been hanging around outside this house before the robbery, now why would he write that? Why would anyone, unless they were trying to tell us something to help Gramps?"

At that point, Norris wailed loudly making everyone turn round.

"Norris," said Stella, "was this you?"

Norris meowed loudly in reply, rubbing himself up against her legs, purring.

"Now this is getting weird," cried Greg. "Cats can't…can't write…they're just cats."

Mildred looked down at Norris and something in her eyes told him she was beginning to waver. "I never trusted Noreen or Frank, and Dad never liked her, he called her an interfering old bitch, well, not when Mum was listening, but I heard him say that more than once."

"Come on!" cried Greg. "What evidence do you have that your aunt and uncle have anything to do with any robbery, let alone the one your dad's just been nicked for…and if you think a cat can…"

"Just believe me, Dad," interrupted Stella. "Norris is no ordinary cat. He helped me escape last night, and if it weren't for him showing up at that flat, I would still be there and if you don't start asking them questions then I will."

"You're not going anywhere," yelled Greg. "You should never have brought her here, Mildred, anything could have happened to her and I'm calling the police, now. Stella, you need to tell me the address of this flat, I'm going round there right now."

"No Dad, you can't, it's not safe..."

"You stay here with your mum. Mildred, make sure she doesn't go out. If anyone tackles Noreen and Frank, it will be me."

As Stella cuddled Norris in her arms, he could sense how tense she suddenly became, her heart beating faster. He doubted Roger would still be there. Any injury he'd sustained would be minor, but Stella couldn't know that. They'd not hung around long enough for him to regain consciousness.

Stella told Greg the address. It was ingrained in Norris' memory, but he was impressed Stella had made a mental note of it. Greg bounded down the stairs and a few seconds later the front door slammed shut.

"Mum, we have to speak to Noreen and Frank, what if they made Gramps do it, threatened him somehow? The police need to know, if he helps them, the police might let him go."

Norris nuzzled Stella's arm, he felt them shaking, heard the tremble in her words, but he also knew Jimmy wasn't going anywhere. He took a firearm to a robbery, there was no way the police would let him go.

"Leave it to your dad, and when he gets back, we'll see about contacting the police, but they'd want to know everything about your kidnapper and how you got away. I know you're tired, love, you've been through an awful thing, but you do need to tell us how you did get away, the police will ask anyway."

"I don't want to talk about that Mum, I'm home, that's all that matters." Stella squeezed Norris tighter.

Of course, Norris knew why Stella didn't want to say too much, it would mean admitting what she did to Roger and there was always the possibility she'd hit him just a bit too hard. It wouldn't be the first time a strike to the back of the head had killed a man. Norris had seen it with his own eyes, a rock to the back of the head had spilt the brains of a young German soldier, left a pool of blood soaking into the parched soil. Jimmy and Norris had watched in horror as the man, surely no older than themselves, had died in front of their very eyes before he could even utter a word. If the war had taught them anything, it was that life could be snuffed out in a second, that there was no time to evaluate, or even see it as an act of killing, it was just the cold-blooded act of survival. There was not a single drop of blood on Roger, and Norris doubted Stella was strong enough to crack open a skull, but for her too, it was an impulsive act of survival, one he knew all too well.

"You wait here today; we'll talk again when your dad gets back. I need to make a phone call." Mildred put her arm around Stella and hugged her before going back downstairs.

Stella turned to face the bathroom mirror again. "I know you wrote this," she said, scooping out the stub of lipstick from the sink. "You're a lot cleverer than they can imagine." She held Norris up and turned him to face her. "You know a lot more, don't you? You've been listening. Did Gramps mean to take you on that robbery or were you trying to stop him?"

Her fingers were digging into the skin under Norris' legs, and he wriggled a little to make her pop him down onto the floor. With Mildred downstairs and Greg out of the house, this was his chance to try to tell Stella more. He lifted his head, looking up at her, and let out a long wail, then, nudging her leg with his paw he led her into Jimmy's room.

"You got something to show me?" asked Stella, following. Downstairs, Norris could hear Mildred talking to someone, it sounded like she was in the kitchen on the other side of the house. He crawled under Jimmy's bed and again he shunted the typewriter out from underneath and sat looking at it, pleading Stella with his eyes to understand what he was asking her. When she didn't say anything, he tapped the keys with his paws, sending letters jolting to the ribbon.

"You want to tell me something else, don't you?"

Norris meowed in agreement.

"Wait a minute, there's no paper." Stella opened the flap of Jimmy's bureau and searched the alcoves. When she failed to find any paper, she opened the drawers of the bureau below until she found a folder full of clean white paper. She retrieved one sheet and quickly fed it into the typewriter and lowered the bar which held the paper in place and then waited.

Norris made himself comfortable in front of the typewriter and began typing. When he'd finished there were a few lines on the paper; it was only the very beginning of what he wanted to say, his heart pounded in his chest and his paws ached but the look on Stella's face made a surge of achievement, which filled him with pride. A tear ran down Stella's face.

"In another life I knew Jimmy, he was my friend. I owe him and he needs our help.
Are you with me?"

She nodded and planted a kiss on the top of Norris' head.

Chapter Thirty-Eight

Norris continued typing.

"We need to go to Noreen and Frank's bungalow; I will lead you there. But first you need to call the police so they can meet us there..."

With Norris tucked under her arm, Stella crept down the stairs, along the hall and out of the front door, leaving Mildred mid-argument with someone on the phone, Noreen by the sound of it. Greg had still not returned, probably he was still at the flat of Roger's aunt. Norris hoped all Greg would find was a locked flat. Stella carried Norris, listening to his meows which told her which way to turn next. They'd headed along Grantchester Road and through a housing estate and this was their first stop. A red phone box stood on the corner of the street, its glass defaced with spray paint and its interior reeking of cheap lager and piss. Stella lifted the receiver and dialled 999.

"Police please," she said. A few seconds later she spoke again. "I know the identity of the gang behind the jewellery shop robberies. I can take you to a property which contains proof they were involved."

Norris' paws ached from all the typing and his back paw still throbbed, swollen now from his fall and instinctively he knew it was probably broken, but there had been no time to communicate that to Stella. Writing was exhausting and he could well see why cats didn't bother with that sort of thing.

The phone call finished, Stella continued on her walk, back down to Grantchester Road and along the route Norris had walked himself before. Passers-by stared at the girl carrying a vocal cat, indeed one woman stopped them.

"Is it hurt?" she asked, reaching out to stroke Norris' head, her thin head tied up in a floral headscarf, her kind eyes peering at them from behind wide tortoiseshell glasses.

"I'm just returning him to his owner," said Stella. "He was lost, that's all. We're okay, thank you."

"He's lucky you found him," said the lady smiling, before continuing on her way along the pavement.

Norris was impressed at how naturally Stella could lie. Though he wasn't so sure he was lucky Stella had found him in that cat rescue centre, he'd grown to love her dearly.

They were outside Noreen's bungalow now, but they held back, far enough away so that Noreen wouldn't see them if she happened to look out of the window to the road. A familiar car was parked outside on her drive and on a glance towards the window of Noreen's sitting room, Norris spotted the all too familiar outline of Roger, his arms gesticulating as if he were arguing. Stella must have seen him too, for she withdrew, further away from the drive and ducked down below a neighbour's fence, holding Norris close to her chest, her arms firmly wrapped around him. There they waited, for what seemed like minutes.

"I hope you're right about this, Norris," she whispered. "That bloke's there and if he sees me now…"

Norris meowed. He couldn't believe his luck that when the police car arrived, they would find not only one of the gang members, but the kidnapper too, who Stella could identify and the fact he was still walking probably meant she wouldn't have to admit to assaulting him either. Maybe, this life wasn't so shitty, after all.

Five minutes later, they heard the sirens before they saw the police cars hurtling down the road behind them. Curtains didn't twitch, but in an area like that, Norris knew it was nothing noteworthy at all. Stella stood up and carried Norris up to the driveway of Noreen's bungalow where the first car, its blue lights still flashing, blockaded in Roger's car so he couldn't get away.

"Are you Stella?" asked a policewoman heading over to where Stella stood, the ginger cat held tightly in her arms.

"Yes," said Stella. "Noreen is inside, so too the evidence I told you about and also a man called Roger, he kidnapped me two days ago and held me in a flat until I escaped last night."

The policewoman didn't look at Stella as she explained, she was staring instead at Norris, who stared back, his head at an angle, trying really hard to form a smile with his face though he reckoned it probably came across as a cat grimacing in pain, so he meowed softly instead.

"This is Norris," said Stella.

"I think we've already met," said the policewoman. "Is that the cat that was found at the scene of the robbery?"

Stella nodded.

"This could get nasty, you're best to stay back but on no account are you to leave here, do you hear me? We need you to make a statement down the station and we need one of your parents to join us."

Again, Stella nodded, then she buried her face in Norris' fur, and she squeezed him tighter still. Mildred would have more than a few words to say about that and with what Stella had done behind her back, so too would Greg. Norris purred softly and then licked Stella's hands gently. He wished with all his heart that he could say something to reassure her, tell her she'd done the right thing for her and for Jimmy. More than ever, he hated being stuck in a cat's body, with no hands with which to gently hold hers, no arms to wrap around her, no strength to give her when hers may yet fail her when she had to face Noreen and Roger as they were, minutes later, escorted out of the bungalow in handcuffs and led towards the waiting police cars.

"It's that bloody cat again!" shrieked Noreen, as she was pushed down into the seat of the police car. "And as for you," she spat towards Roger, who was being led by two policemen towards the second police car. "This is all your fault, it was your idea, I just went along with it."

The car doors slammed and the two police cars drove away. Stella and Norris were left with the policewoman who held in her hand a clear evidence bag inside which lay the tub of face cream which concealed the ruby ring.

"We'll call your mum and dad on the way to the police station, but your cat there, it will have to travel in the back of the van."

Norris saw Spike being dragged into the back of a

police transit van and he remembered the police pound he'd ended up in after the robbery.

"No!" cried Stella. "He stays with me. If it weren't for him, you'd never have caught those responsible. And don't forget Frank or his friend Ernie, I told you about them."

"You leave the rest of it to the professionals," said the policewoman. "Now let's get in, shall we?"

Sitting in the back of the police car, with Norris ensconced on her lap, Stella planted another kiss on the top of Norris' head. "That's a thank you from Gramps," she said.

Chapter Thirty-Nine

The police interview room was bare but for a small table in the middle and five hard plastic chairs. The walls were painted a herby green and the air smelt of sweat and desperation. Norris sat curled up on Stella's lap, his belly full, at last, after the custody sergeant had insisted Norris be given a saucer of milk and the tuna turfed out from the inside of a limp canteen sandwich. Stella sat with Mildred on one side of her and Greg on the other. The policewoman, who'd met Stella at Noreen's bungalow, sat across the table, a sheaf of papers before her and a reassuringly large smile on her face. Norris wondered if this had been the very same interview room in which Jimmy would have sat, not so very long ago.

"My name is Inspector Willoughby. I have to say this is the first time I've ever had a cat in my interview room, and it is probably against my better judgement to have one now."

Norris sat up straight and watched the Inspector closely as she lay four photographs out on the table in front of them depicting Noreen, Frank, Ernie and Roger.

"Can you confirm if you recognise these individuals?"

"That's my aunt, Noreen, and her husband Frank," said Mildred, pointing to two of the pictures. "Noreen was my mum's sister."

"What makes you think they may have been involved in the armed robberies of a string of jewellery shops?"

"Noreen had a ring from the things stolen, in her

bathroom," said Stella.

"I can confirm that we found that item as and where you described it, but what I don't understand, is how you could possibly have known that?" said Inspector Willoughby. "Had you ever been in Noreen's property? Did you see it there yourself?"

"No," said Stella.

"Of course she hadn't," interrupted Mildred. "My daughter has never been in that bungalow, why would she? I couldn't stand my aunt, and I doubt Stella even knew where she lived."

"Mum, I can answer for myself," said Stella

"Carry on," said Inspector Willoughby.

"Norris told me he'd found the ring."

"Oh come on," burst in Greg. "He's a cat! That doesn't make any sense. Cats can't talk, they can't break into houses…you're in shock, after what you've been through."

"Let's try to clarify things, shall we?" said Inspector Willoughby. "You're telling me, Norris here can communicate with you? And that according to your statement he not only found you at the address Roger Donaldson had held you, against your will, but had also delivered a note to Roger there and then, he subsequently showed you where Noreen lived after describing what she'd hidden in her bathroom? Is that correct?"

"Yes, it is," said Stella,

"I told you, Greg," said Mildred, "there's something about that cat, something special."

Norris had sat and listened patiently but now he jumped up onto the interview table, padded over to the photographs and sat down right on top of the picture of Noreen. He looked at each and every one of them around the table and meowed loudly.

"There must be something I'm missing here," said Inspector Willoughby, allowing herself to reach out a hand and stroke Norris' head. "I've no idea how a cat can communicate ideas like that, or how he could possibly know Noreen, Ernie, Frank and Roger were involved in any criminal activity but..."

Norris pricked up his ears and turned to face the Inspector. He could see it from her point of view, even Mildred's and Greg's for that matter. He looked like a rather ordinary ginger cat and he most definitely couldn't speak human but what the Inspector said next, took him by surprise.

"But, I have to admit there is some evidence which makes me wonder what the truth really could be."

She produced a copy of the local newspaper, dated the day before and turned to page five. Under the headline, "*Cat travels the evening bus*", was a picture of Norris sitting beside a lady on the seat of a bus.

"How often do you see a cat travelling by bus?" asked the Inspector. "Indeed, how often do cats attend the scene of a robbery? I would put it all down to coincidence, if we hadn't received a statement from Jimmy's solicitor. It seems he's broken his silence. He has not only verified your evidence, that he was taken on by Frank and Ernie to be the driver for a robbery but that he had not taken Norris here along for the ride. He claims the cat smuggled itself into his car, then the getaway car and then knocked his gun out of his hand, in what appeared to be a deliberate act."

Norris meowed loudly and Mildred and Greg looked totally astonished.

"Now, when everything points in one direction, and even if it sounds totally implausible, well, I'm inclined to consider it may actually be the case," said the Inspector. "There are those who will have us believe cats are far more intelligent than we realise. But what I don't understand, is how this cat communicated any of this to you, Stella."

"My lipstick on the mirror!" exclaimed Mildred. "And he wanted me to read the newspaper article about the robberies, the one I'd thrown away in the bin."

"That's because Norris was trying to warn us Gramps was involved in something criminal, but you wouldn't listen, Mum. I wouldn't listen at first," said Stella, "not until he saved me from that flat."

"All of you, really!" cried Greg. "You can't seriously believe that cat really did anything…knew anything…it's ridiculous! This is a complete farce!" He threw his hands up in the air and pushed back his chair.

"I can prove it," cried Stella. "Norris typed it all up on Gramps' old typewriter, the note for Roger, the explanation to me, the directions, all of it."

"A cat, typing! That's insane!" cried Greg.

"Is it really?" said Mildred. "Stella wouldn't lie, not like you. She's decent and honest…"

"Well that pretty well makes her the only one in your family then."

"Don't say that…" began Mildred.

"Let's have quiet now, can we," interrupted Inspector Willowby.

And as every human around the table questioned how

a simple cat like Norris could ever have done such a thing, Norris was still trying to understand whose idea it was to put a human, who'd lived eight unremarkable lives, into a cat's body and then chuck him into a quagmire of emotions and moral dilemmas just to see what would happen. It really didn't matter if anyone in that room believed him now, because Jimmy had admitted his involvement in a criminal act and now only the mercy of the legal process could save him from living out his days in a prison cell.

"I thank you for your co-operation," resumed the Inspector. "If we need more information, we'll be in touch."

"Is that it?" asked Stella. "What about the robbers and Roger? Will you charge them? Will they let my Gramps go, they made him, they must have done."

"As I said, that's all for now, you can go home and take your cat with you. Oh, and I wouldn't say anything about what you've told me about Norris to any of the journalists who are probably camped outside the police station right now, because if you do, everyone in the country is going to want that cat, the media will be trying to interview him on breakfast telly!"

And Inspector Willoughby wasn't wrong. Greg and Mildred had to smuggle Stella and Norris out of a rear door from the station to avoid the huge crowd of journalists that had amassed outside the police station, plus the TV crews who hoped for an interview, any interview, with the owners of the cat who was not only taken to an armed robbery and rode on buses but had also been the very first cat to be interviewed at a police station.

A waiting police car drove them home, but the news had travelled fast and journalists were camped out on their front lawn. The car took them down the track and round the back, past Boris who sat on the wall watching them as they disembarked and hurried in through the back garden gate into the garden of number fifty-four Grantchester Road.

Safely indoors and huddled around the kitchen table, Greg exclaimed, "Now everyone's going to want a bloody ginger cat, as if somehow, they're special."

And Norris remembered his chat with Boris. Boris wasn't ginger, he was tortoiseshell and he, too, was living out some kind of warped atonement game for his life's misdeeds. Maybe it wasn't ginger cats who were special, hell, maybe cats weren't special at all, but they were all not what their owners imagined them to be?

Chapter Forty

It didn't take long for the police to take action, and Norris knew he should have been grateful that it was his actions which led to the police's breakthrough in their hunt for the rest of the jewellery shop gang. That evening Mildred, Greg and Stella had watched the night time local news, Greg and Mildred once again back to different chairs and Stella curled up on the sofa with Norris close beside her. The first news headline was probably the best they could have hoped for.

"Police have arrested four other members of a criminal gang believed to have been responsible for the raids on a number of high street jewellery shops."

No names had been released, but that was only to be expected. It was the following news story which made Norris' fur bristle, seeing a picture of himself on the bus, other snaps of him trotting along Grantchester Road. An interview with a man outside the police station revealed a ginger cat had been taken into the police station, but the police were unwilling to confirm whether it was in connection with their ongoing enquiries or whether it was the same cat which had allegedly been found at the scene of one of the robberies. Stella reached over to Norris and stroked him gently. In all the lives that had come before, he'd never been worthy of inclusion in any newspaper story and now it seemed he was notorious.

"Great," said Greg. "A famous cat, everyone will want

him or a piece of him…but maybe we can capitalise on it…you know, sell our story, take him on chat shows, I bet they'll pay."

"Dad! How could you even suggest it?"

"We'll do no such thing," snapped Mildred. "That's Stella's cat, you keep well away from him."

"So how do you think you're going to keep this house then?" said Greg, leaning across to Mildred. "I doubt it's paid for, and with your dad banged up inside, your wages won't pay for it."

"Maybe the mortgage is already paid," said Mildred, "either way it's no concern of yours."

Norris remembered the letter Jimmy had begun to type, the one which still lay under his bed where Norris had left it.

"But Gramps will be coming home soon," cried Stella. "Once the police realise none of it was his idea, he'll be home again, won't he Mum?"

Mildred put down her mug of hot chocolate on the arm of her chair and the pause in her response said exactly what Norris was already thinking.

"I'm not sure it's that simple, we'll have to wait and see."

"But…" began Stella.

"Armed robbers don't get to go home," said Greg, "not even if they dob in their mates."

Mildred flashed Greg a glare, but it was too late. Stella's face crumpled. She bundled Norris up in her arms and ran upstairs to her room. Norris could hear the cut of Mildred's voice in the room below them but not the actual words as his head was muffled in Stella's tight embrace, her tears dripping on his fur as her shoulders shuddered with each sob.

It wasn't how Norris had naively hoped this scenario would have played out. Any idea he once fleetingly had that his new life was an opportunity to make amends, evaporated just as surely as water runs out of a hole in the bottom of a bucket. Worst still, was that he'd punctured it himself. If Jimmy did come home, it would be after a stretch inside and who knew how long that might be or even if he'd live to see a release date. Everything Norris had done, or tried to do, had failed to alter the outcome, as if it were pre-ordained and Norris had just been made a pawn in this game of life. And then another awful realisation made his stomach tumble, maybe this life really was a punishment for his failings as a human being, maybe this was the hell that some believed in, the opposite of a heaven, the fire and damnation. Maybe just like Boris, this was Norris' penance. Boris had to watch a daughter struggle in a life without her mother, powerless to make amends. Must Norris too watch the rest of Jimmy's life be snatched away and his family fall apart without him? After all Norris had done to help Stella, her heart was still breaking, and just as with his own daughter, Janice, there was nothing he could do.

He waited until everyone slept, then he padded down the stairs, across the kitchen and out of the cat flap. He stood in the cold grass. Clouds scuttled across the face of a nearly full moon casting an eerie glow across the lawn. There Norris sat, scanning the night sky above him until the clouds drifted apart revealing a small spattering of stars. If he were looking for a sign, one never came and after a few minutes the sound of something small moving through the grass near him made him look down. A small mouse stalled, its whiskers picked out in the moonlight, its eyes bright. Other cats may have taken the easy prey but Norris watched it slink away deeper into the garden of weeds and out of sight. He didn't much like being a cat, he didn't have the heart or the will to embrace it, even if it were the only life he had left. Jimmy had effectively gone from his life, awaiting his destiny in a cell, not unlike the incarceration he must have endured in the prison camp all those years ago and on that cold October night, Norris couldn't envisage how to continue at all. Never before had he reached such an absolute helplessness. In previous lives, if things didn't go the way he thought they should, he'd change tack, change job, change lover, change city even, but now where else was there to go? He could embrace the life of a cat, and the killer instinct inside that he knew only too well, live wild in the outskirts of the town or hitch a lift to the country and live near a farm, but that would mean walking away from Stella, a girl he'd grown to love, to care about. If he couldn't save Jimmy, maybe instead he could protect his granddaughter, repay his debt that way? But the family dynamics playing out between Mildred and Greg made him uneasy and his unexpected fame made him even more nervous of Greg, who had surely seen the opportunity of making Norris a commodity, a means of making money.

Unable to settle in the chill of the night, Norris left the garden and headed down the track that led to Grantchester Road, his leg now lame, his foot an impediment to any kind of speed. He wondered if eventually Stella and Mildred would take him once again to the vet but they were so embroiled in the police involvement and the fate of Jimmy, that Norris had no idea how long it might be before they realised his pain.

Out on Grantchester Road, he walked along to the garden of number fifty-two, the home of Boris and he jumped over the small wall, limping down the path that led around the side of the house. He never imagined he'd want to seek out Boris, but like it or not they had a tie, a shared experience, and now when all else seemed lost, Norris wanted to talk to someone who just might understand. As a man he'd had few close friends, didn't share feelings or fears, just bravado and false optimism and overinflated successes, like big kids boasting in the playground. It was Jimmy who he'd talked to a few times, when the uncertainty of war and the longing to be anywhere else had got the better of him and he'd let down his guard. And Jimmy didn't mock him, but quietly nodded, as if he understood and now Norris couldn't even say sorry for all he should have done if only he'd had the bravery in his heart that all soldiers were meant to have.

At first there was no sign of Boris, but then Norris saw his eyes staring out at him from under a rhododendron bush. Norris inched closer.

"The famous cat," meowed Boris, standing up and padding out from underneath the dried brown flower heads. "I saw you on the telly, I hope it all works out, but a word of warning..." Boris now stood in front of Norris, their noses nearly touching. "As cats, we're meant to blend in, humans respect cats because they're aloof, independent, clever, but careful not to get too close or too dependent on their owners because, mate, we were just like them. We know how flawed humans are. Watch and observe for sure, but if you get too emotionally involved, you'll only make things worse for yourself. You can't change what humans choose to do, yeah, this life is rubbing our noses into all we cocked up, but like all lives, it's our life, use it for yourself, mate, we can't undo the past."

But that was just it, Norris needed to undo what he'd done but Boris was right, no matter what he'd tried, he'd failed and maybe that had been the whole point.

"I need to make Jimmy realise I'm sorry, if I can communicate with Stella, why can't I..."

"Now look here, what did you just say?"

Norris thought of the notes he'd typed for Stella, but he also remembered how long it had taken to persuade her to listen to him at all, to consider for even one moment that a cat had anything to say.

"I typed up what I wanted to say to Stella and..."

"Then type a letter to this Jimmy, if it's so important to you, and then move on. Being a cat's not so bad, humans dote on you, feed you, meet your every basic need. There's no need to work, no debts, no stress, mate. Relax, enjoy this life more, it makes the regret easier, I can assure you. Chase the female cats, there's lots to be had...but by the look of you, you have too much of a conscience, that's probably how you ended up in this life in the first place. Me, yeah, I hate what I did, makes it hard to stomach being here, but if I live out this life, maybe I'll get another."

Norris didn't want another and prayed this was his

last. Now the idea had been seeded, it grew in his mind all the way back to number fifty-four Grantchester Road and his seat next to the sitting room window. He'd get Stella to help him type and send a letter to Jimmy. But not from Norris the cat, from Norris the friend, the friend who should have saved him.

Chapter Forty-One

Today was the day Norris was going to say the things he should have had the courage to say years ago, in another life. He'd stayed awake all night, crafting that apology in his head, only next morning Stella was nowhere to be found, and Mildred had cornered Greg in the kitchen and was shouting at him as she waved a piece of burnt toast.

"It's time you left, I should never have let you stay, it's not a week and already you've belittled me, confused Stella and you tried to use her cat as a means to make money…and it's going to stop, today!" cried Mildred, grabbing her mug of tea so that it slopped over the side of the mug and dripped onto her white blouse.

"I'm not confusing her, I'm her father or have you conveniently forgotten that, that we are still married…I have just as much right to say what happens regarding her as you do."

"Oh, no you don't, you gave up that right when you started shagging girls half your age and…"

"It was just a mid-life crisis, you know that, it was a mistake. You and Stella are my life, I thought we'd moved on, got closer, you know, that despite what your old man did, we were working together again, for Stella."

Mildred bust out laughing, tossed the last of her tea down the sink and took a loud crunch of her toast.

"I'm off to work and when I get back you'd better be gone. And no hanging around here to catch Stella at lunchtime either. Today's going to be hard enough for her at school as it is."

"You can't stop me seeing my daughter, not like last time."

"She's old enough to decide if she wants to see you, so let her be the judge of that," said Mildred, her voice calmer now.

Norris stayed by the open door, not wanting to disturb what looked like a pivotal moment for Mildred. It seemed he hadn't been the only one preparing words last night. He wondered what had shifted to give Mildred the confidence that had now left Greg flushed, droplets of sweat forming on his forehead.

"Get your bag packed and leave, now, I can't be late for work today." Mildred took a dishcloth from beside the sink, rinsed it under the tap, wrung it out then dabbed at the stain on the front of her blouse. "I've got an interview for a promotion today, supervisor no less, the extra money will be just in time. Five minutes and I'll be locking up, best you hurry."

Mildred dumped the cloth in a heap next to the tap and walked out of the kitchen, straight past Norris and into the hall. Greg dithered for a moment by the table, then he kicked its leg and strode out of the kitchen, pushing past Norris. Norris took this as his cue to exit through the cat flap and out into the garden. He didn't need to witness the last scene, the dying embers of a doomed relationship, he'd played that out in numerous variations with wives he'd either fallen out of love with, those he should never have married and one he despised so much by the end, that he couldn't stomach his cornflakes in the morning with her verbal diarrhoea exploding over the breakfast table at him. No, he knew how Mildred may have been feeling and hoped Greg had enough brains to give up on her, at least for now. Norris knew only too well that a woman's raw emotions left no room for a man's feelings. But it was Stella that he worried about, though he'd never worried enough about his own children to feel what he felt for Stella now. His heart ached, she'd been through enough, more than enough and though last night he'd watched her sleep, stroked her hand with his head, it could never, ever be enough.

Now, Norris made his way down the track and back up to Grantchester Road, the morning air heavy, the clouds sodden with rain yet to fall. His paw, though still painful to walk on, took his weight better, so maybe he hadn't broken it after all. He rounded the corner to see Mildred heading along the road towards the bus stop and Greg walking in the opposite direction towards town, his shoulders slumped, hands deep in his pockets, a heavy bag dragging him down on one side. Norris was too distracted watching them going their separate ways to notice the person whose hands now swiped at his fur.

"Hey, that's the cat from the telly!" came the voice, followed by another. "Grab it!"

Norris hissed, ruffling his fur along his back like a teenager attempting a Mohican with hair gel, then he lashed out at the hand which had so nearly caught hold of him.

"Arghh! The spiteful shit tried to bite me!"

"What did you expect?" laughed the other boy who pulled a faced at Norris whilst trying not to laugh. "It's a criminal cat, hard as your old man, I reckon."

Norris darted between them, along the pavement and then down a footpath and across a well-manicured lawn dotted with a collection of gaudy coloured garden gnomes. He buried underneath a leylandii which had already grown so tall it obscured the garden beyond. He curled up into a ball, hoping to sleep and failing. When the rain came, it fell in sheets, louder than the sound of the morning traffic and the voices of the boys who'd at first given chase before deciding better of it. There Norris stayed. The rain stopped and the wind picked up, seeking him out under the branches, huddled between the hedge's fragrant green fronds. Minutes dragged into an hour before he slunk out from underneath the hedge and into the garden now saturated and cold underfoot.

Norris headed back onto the road and along to number fifty-two, nosing first around the garden, then trotting along the path that led to the back of the house. There was no sign of Boris. He realised he didn't know what he had to say, even had he found him. He was heading back to the road again when he paused. He wondered what the woman Boris lived with looked like, and to satisfy his curiosity, Norris headed over to the bay window which looked over the front garden. He jumped up onto the window ledge and peered inside, beyond the plaid curtains tied back with cord into the yellow painted sitting room beyond. On a burgundy velour armchair sat a woman in her early thirties maybe, neat auburn bob, trim arms and legs, dressed in jeans and a bright orange jumper. On her lap, stretched out, lay Boris. The tortoiseshell cat rubbed his head against the woman's hand that stroked him, his front legs wrapped around her other arm in an embrace. Despite Boris's hard exterior, his puffed-up bravado, here with his owner, it was as if he'd melted into a devoted feline, giving as much affection as he received, to the woman whose mother he had killed. The affection looked so natural, Norris knew it was real, no matter what Boris had said. He'd accepted this new life, was living it. Maybe it was time Norris conceded he must do the same. Stella needed him and he knew he needed her, surely that had to be enough and maybe it would be if he could just talk to Jimmy, even if it were only the one time.

It was nearly lunchtime according to the clock on the sitting room wall. Norris sat on the windowsill waiting. When he saw Stella he jumped down and headed up to the front door to greet her. The door opened and Stella stepped inside, shrugging off her coat. She looked exhausted and the mascara she must have applied after leaving the house that morning to evade Mildred, was smudged under her eyes like two fat bruises. She'd been crying.

"Norris, it's you." She crouched down, dropping her bag on the hall floor and bundled Norris into a hug which squeezed his ribs. "I bet Mum didn't feed you properly, let's see what we can find."

But I need to tell you something, meowed Norris but, of course, she couldn't understand him, even now, so Norris let her carry him into the kitchen. He waited patiently as she fed him a tin of tuna and a saucer of milk. Despite Mildred's initial resistance to giving

Norris treats, she seemed to have softened. The cupboard had a stack of tuna tins and he'd never seen Mildred eat any, or Jimmy for that matter. He had to admit, since Jimmy's arrest, Mildred had changed, her bond with Stella growing, her new independence from Greg making her a woman Norris thought he could grow to get used to. His appetite sated, Norris rubbed himself up against Stella's legs, meowing incessantly.

"You can't still be hungry," laughed Stella, stroking the top of his head.

Norris meowed louder, this time leading her to the kitchen door.

"You've got something to say, haven't you?" said Stella, following him out into the hall and then up the stairs. "Sometimes I wonder who you really are."

It was something Norris had struggled with, the idea that maybe now he could tell her his story, but it was more bizarre than anything he'd revealed so far and the risk that Stella night reject him was too much to bear. The letter he needed to type would say enough, for now anyway.

With the typewriter back in place and the paper inserted, Norris knew he needed to give Stella clear instructions first, for the letter he would be typing had to be sent to Jimmy in prison, sealed so Mildred didn't read it.

Ten minutes later, his paws already aching from typing out instructions, Stella bent down and kissed his head.

"I wonder how many secrets you really have," she whispered. "You saved me and I trust you but none of this makes any sense. Why would you want to write to

Gramps in prison, how could he ever have known you before?"

Of course, Norris knew the letter would reveal enough to answer some of her questions, but it was Jimmy he was writing to, and he had to just get down what he needed to say, quickly and in a few words, in case Jimmy couldn't bear to read anymore. So Norris began typing on a fresh sheet of paper.

"Jimmy, I should have written to you so many years ago but I was a coward, I couldn't find the words and didn't think you'd want to hear them anyway.

I never should have left you like that back in France. I should have done all I could to save you. I am embarrassed to say, I was scared, too scared to stay or to fight. All I could see was a way out for me in the seconds I had to decide. I am ashamed, I always have been. I deeply regret letting you down. I won't ask for forgiveness because I don't deserve it, but I am truly sorry.

Your friend, Norris

Chapter Forty-Two

Somehow just writing the letter had been cathartic, seeing the words in black and white, the words Norris hoped Jimmy would read, they had lifted a heaviness from his heart. Maybe that was why some people went to confession, to unburden their soul. Until yesterday, Norris had never told anyone what he had done back in France, not his unit, his new wife, nor any of the acquaintances he had later called friends. Instead, the guilt had grown inside him just like the cancer which riddled his body in his early sixties, killing him within just a few years. He spent the rest of the day sleeping, too exhausted to even pad out into the garden or watch life roll by through the window. He'd felt Stella's presence beside him, the reassuring warmth of her body never far away from the sofa where he slept. It was Mildred coming home which woke him.

"Stella, set the table, we're celebrating."

Norris smelt the tang of vinegar on freshly fried chips and followed Stella into the kitchen.

Mildred unwrapped huge portions of fish and chips, transferring them to plates before setting them down on the table.

"I got that promotion, it was barely an interview, just a little chat really. Supervisor, can you believe it? I start next week. You should have seen the other girls, envious or what."

"That's brilliant, Mum." Stella squeezed a large dollop of ketchup onto her chips. "Where's Dad?"

"Gone," said Mildred.

"Oh," said Stella, pushing a chip around her plate.

Mildred picked up a large flake of cod and dropped it on the floor to where Norris sat listening. "I don't want him here."

"That's okay, Mum, I understand. Could I post a letter to Gramps?" Stella placed the letter Norris had typed, now in a sealed white envelope, onto the table. "I'll need the address."

Mildred put down her fork and placed her hand over Stella's.

"That's a lovely thing to do," she said. "He'll appreciate that. We might even visit him soon, if I can make the arrangements. I'll pop the address on for you and put it in the post tomorrow on my way to work."

"He won't really be in prison that long, will he, Mum? Dad said…you know…helping the police wouldn't really make all that much difference."

Norris pricked up his ears, but he'd already guessed what was coming.

"I'm really sorry, Stella. But it will be months before the trial and it's very likely that because your grandad took a gun to the robbery, he will receive quite a lengthy sentence. I'm sorry, I know it's not what you want to hear but we'll stay here, and we'll visit him."

Stella didn't reply, just ate the rest of her chips in between silent sobs. When Mildred had finished eating, Stella scraped the rest of her fish into Norris' bowl.

It seemed Frank, Ernie, Noreen and Roger were as bad at covering their criminal tracks as Jimmy had been at choosing acquaintances. It wasn't long before their faces appeared on the news and in the local papers.

All of them were in prison on remand awaiting trial. Norris' notoriety died down much to his relief, though Mildred had to refuse two TV appearances, including one for the breakfast chat show. Norris wondered what had happened to Spike. He remembered the night he'd spent in the police dog pound but, of course, it was unlikely anyone would be heading there to claim the terrier and Norris couldn't help but feel responsible, albeit only briefly.

It was a couple of weeks before a letter arrived addressed to Stella, written in spidery handwriting and marked, "Her Majesty's Prison Service". Mildred handed it to Stella at breakfast just before she had to leave for school. There hadn't been time to open it, so it had lain on the little cabinet next to Stella's bed all morning. In his letter to Jimmy, Norris had added a postscript:

"Please send any reply c/o Stella."

He'd added it as an afterthought in case Jimmy wondered how Norris had tracked him down.

Norris curled up on Stella's pillow, her bear nuzzled between his paws. He stared at the envelope for almost an hour solid, his breathing heavy, his heart a racing thump. He'd never expected a reply and now that it sat there, so very near but impossible to open, Norris began to dread what was inside. But whatever was inside, it had been Norris who had prompted it, so he only had himself to blame. If he'd been in Jimmy's shoes, he'd probably have binned it or burnt it, but then he remembered Jimmy didn't have those options, not now.

An uneasiness turned to queasiness and Norris jumped down from the bed and headed outside hoping the chill air would help clear his head. A weak sun tried to warm his fur as he sat upon the back garden wall looking out over the backs of terraces that made up Jimmy's street. He felt more inclined to stay now Greg was gone but he doubted he could take the mundaneness of it all, the limited horizons of being a cat. The irony wasn't lost on him that throughout his human lives he'd pondered why cats just seemed to sit there, looking over gardens or out of windows but, of course, now he knew they were probably reflecting on what had come before and what had really brought them to that point in their lives, maybe, like him, they were wondering if they'd done something differently, would they be there now? Was Jimmy the only reason he was sat there, watching people putting out their bins or hanging out washing, or smoking a cigarette in the remnants of autumn? Or had a whole multitude of sins made up his score sheet and singled him out. He thought of the wives he neglected, the men he'd cheated, the many occasions where he'd promised to be there for his children only to find more interesting things to do instead. The presents he gave instead of his time, the lies that had been too easy to tell, the people whose dreams he'd trodden on to get where he'd wanted to go. Were they why he had nothing but the fur upon his back and the love of one young girl?

"Don't do it," came the voice of Boris.

The tortoiseshell cat sat on the track below him. Norris looked down.

"I tried all of that, it doesn't get you anywhere." Boris leapt up onto the wall and settled down beside Norris, like two old men sharing a bench at the seaside, reminiscing on days gone by.

"Stop doing what?" meowed Norris, not sure he wanted company.

"Dwelling, postulating, identifying, evaluating all you must have done wrong to be here today. I did it and did it change anything? No. Did it make it easier to bear this life? No."

"But I can't help it," replied Norris. His mind still fixated on that envelope, the only remaining link between his life and Jimmy's.

"We can't change what happened, not really."

"We can try," meowed Norris.

"I looks like you already have. But if you think throwing yourself off balconies and unnecessarily drawing attention to yourself will really make any difference, I think you're wrong."

"What did you try to do?" meowed Norris, because it would seem this kind of viewpoint could only come from someone who'd tried just that and failed.

Boris sprawled on the top of the wall, flicking the tip of his tail. "I tried to show her what had happened, part of me hoping I'd die in the process, but the car screeched to a halt breaking only my left leg. If you look closely, you can see it never properly straightened, the bones didn't knit together as they should have."

"So, you killed her mother…with your car?" meowed

Norris.

"Hit and run, they called it. Yes, I hit her. I was well over the limit, but I didn't see her in time, and I didn't run on purpose, I was shit scared."

"So, it was an accident."

"No, she would have lived apparently, if help had arrived earlier, if I hadn't left the scene on that back road that meant it was over an hour before she was found. She died a week later, I read it in the paper, though of course, I was long gone by then. So you see, I killed her, as good as."

"But what was she doing there, alone?"

"Running away, from someone she thought was worse than me. Her daughter had been staying with a friend, I can only be thankful of that."

"So, what happened to you, after the car hit you?"

"You can work that out surely," meowed Boris. "The silly cow loved me even more, nursed me to health, paid the vet bills she could ill afford. She dotes on me, her own mother's killer, try living with that."

But Norris had seen the affection in the way Boris had lain on his owner's lap, the tenderness.

"So, what are you going to do now?" meowed Boris.

"I haven't decided," replied Norris and he wouldn't have told Boris even if he had.

That lunch time, Stella came home. This time she didn't even think of food, or call Norris, she just bounded up the stairs to her room and sat down on the bed with the letter. Norris leapt up beside her just as she slit the envelope open.

"Meowww!!! Wait for me, why don't you," he yowled

but Stella ignored him and took out the single sheet of paper inside which she spread out on the duvet in front of her so Norris could see. His whole body trembled as he read the words, in the same spidery handwriting as the envelope.

"Dear Norris,

I never stopped wondering what happened to you, how good it is to hear from you. Word got back to me eventually that you'd safely escaped France but of course, by the time I returned at the end of the war I could not trace you.

Why ever are you sorry? It was my stupid idea to go into that barn, I was hungry and I let it cloud my judgement. I walked into a trap and took you with me, I should be the one saying sorry. I should have known it was too dangerous, but you know me, I act without thinking and it looks like I've done it again.

If I ever get out of here, we should catch up.

Your friend,

Jimmy

PS If you know my Stella, which it sounds like you do, keep an eye on her for me.

Chapter Forty-Three

May 2011

By the time Jimmy was released from prison and returned home, he was a very old man indeed, so too was Norris, only his years were counted in cat time. Mildred had kept her promise and lived on in Jimmy's house, waiting for his return. Norris, unlike with his beloved daughter Janice, had been able to watch Stella grow up from troubled teenager to a mature young woman who had since settled in a home of her own. She'd taken Norris with her. In a very modern arrangement, Norris travelled everywhere with her in a rucksack which doubled as a cat carrier of all things. She seemed to sense Norris' need to be with her whenever she travelled. She frequently took him back to Grantchester Road to visit Mildred.

In the intervening years, Norris had typed many a letter and though Stella had read each and every one, he never wrote to her. She seemed to accept who he once was, and however difficult it may have been to comprehend, she'd just accepted it, though she never once mentioned it to Mildred.

One bright day in early May, Stella stowed Norris in his travelling rucksack and took him to fifty-four Grantchester Road, only as they walked up the garden path, he sensed something about that day was different. Stella had squeezed him especially tight and kissed him on the head before helping him inside his carrier and she talked almost incessantly all the way there on the bus as if she were nervous. Now as Mildred opened the door, Norris heard it, the voice of Jimmy Morgan, only now it had a shaky edge to it and each word seemed to take an effort.

"Stella."

A pair of arms were wrapped around her, squeezing the carrier with it.

"Gramps, it's so lovely to have you home. Mum's been fussing for weeks."

"What have you got there?" asked Jimmy.

Norris felt himself being lowered, saw the zip opening and he stepped out onto the hall carpet

"That can't be the same cat, is it?" said Jimmy, staring down at Norris.

When Stella had moved into her own ground floor flat, she'd abandoned cat food altogether much to Norris' relief. Instead, his diet had consisted of tuna, bacon and the occasional fried egg and his waistline had swelled. The last time he'd set eyes on Jimmy, Norris had been a slender ginger cat, now he was solid, with a rotund middle and a gait to match, his face fuller, his fur sprinkled with white hairs. Norris looked up at Jimmy. The intervening years had not been kind, the old man in front of him stood with a pronounced stoop, a walking stick in his hand, the skin almost see-through, it was so thin. Only a few wisps of hair remained on his head and age spots had spread across his forehead, but they were the same eyes and they sparkled with a smile.

"Let's be having you," he said scooping Norris up and carrying him into the sitting room where Mildred had strewn a gaudy 'welcome home' banner across the window. On the table sat a large chocolate cake covered in frosting.

"I'll pop the kettle on," she said, leaving Jimmy with Stella.

There had been days when Norris had wondered if he'd live to see Jimmy again, indeed if Jimmy would ever actually make it home, so it was with the strangest feeling in his tummy that Norris agreed to sit on Jimmy's lap. Once Stella started chatting, she couldn't stop and two cups of tea later, she was still grilling poor Jimmy on his time in Her Majesty's establishment that no-one actually named. Norris was relieved to hear less horror stories than he'd expected and was heartened to hear of how Jimmy had used his time to rediscover reading and working in the prison's small vegetable garden when the opportunity arose.

"But you know what really kept me going in those early bleak years were the letters I received from an old friend of mine."

Norris pricked up his ears and turned to look up at Jimmy as he talked.

"I couldn't believe it when the first one arrived, from someone I'd served with in the army, going way back. I've no idea how he traced me, but I guess making the national papers helped."

Stella just nodded.

"You never really talked about your time back then, Dad," said Mildred, tidying away the empty teacups and sweeping cake crumbs off the cream tablecloth.

"Maybe he didn't want to," chipped in Stella, catching Norris' eye.

Jimmy wouldn't be drawn. "We wrote regularly after

that, for many years, well until I received notice of my release date. I rather hoped I might be able to meet him, but alas the last letter I received was different, the banter had gone, I was worried I'd upset him."

Mildred put her hand on Jimmy's shoulder. "I'm sorry Dad, what did it say?"

"That's just it, it didn't say very much. Let me think…that's it, it simply said, you've made me understand something and for that I will always be grateful. I won't be able to write to you again, but you remain my friend, always."

Stella leaned over and stroked Norris' head. He saw the unshed tear that glistened in her eye. The day Norris had typed that last letter with Stella's help, it was with a new understanding. Their years of correspondence had reminded Norris how close they'd once been, how together they'd faced the awakening of horror. Having enlisted, they'd travelled into a war they were deeply ill-prepared to face. Where once, Norris was convinced he'd failed a dear friend, he grew to realise they had both been floundering in an adult world, a world fraught with danger, never far from death. When Norris had first been re-born a cat and came face to face with Jimmy again, he was ashamed of what had happened, convinced this new life was a penance, retribution for what had come before. But as he'd grown older and he re-discovered their friendship, he realised that though this life was one of forgiveness, it was himself he needed to forgive. Jimmy's and Norris' lives may have diverged, their fortunes very different, but they had shared an experience which had shaped them. Back in France, Norris had lost a comrade, but in the years that followed Jimmy's imprisonment, Norris had gained a friendship that would last until his dying day.

It was six weeks later, cuddled up in his favourite place on Jimmy's lap, as he slumbered in his chair, that was to be his final day of his ninth life, and he knew it would be his last. He had lived all his lives and eventually, he had made his peace. It was time to say goodbye and he was content. In the distance, waiting, he could see his beloved daughter, Janice and that was when he realised that he was walking towards her on two legs, not four and behind him, he left an old man who had been his young friend, stroking a ginger cat as he took his last breath.

About the Author

Dawn Treacher is a recent addition to the growing anthology of authors writing for Provoco Publishing. Joining us in 2023, she has already published The Seeds of Murder and A Deadly Plot with us. These two novels were Dawn's first cosy crime, murder mystery stories for a grown-up audience. Dawn is an established children's book author and illustrator. Her love of crime fiction has seen her embark on a new series of cosy crime mysteries, fuelled by her love of amateur sleuths, gardening, and inspired by the rural North Yorkshire villages in which she has lived over the last twenty years.

In the warmer months she can be found writing in Geraldine, her caravan in the garden. As a carer for her husband, writing has long been her creative outlet in which she supports fellow writers to master, by running creative writing and critique group.

The Ninth Life of Norris is Dawn's first foray into the world of speculative fiction writing, and she has captured the magical realism of the subject with relish, producing an action packed and, somehow, entirely believable tale of a cat who can communicate with humans. She is currently writing her first psychological thriller, due for publication in late 2025. Her books can be found on Amazon and in all good bookstores.

Check out the first of Dawn's murder mystery tales in the Green Fingered Sleuth series!

The Seeds of Murder

He plucked a soft velvet petal and held it close to his nose, its perfume as sweet as the scent of his wife's neck, the pink the same shade as her favourite lipstick. Cedric popped the petal into the top pocket of his corduroy jacket before pushing open the garden gate and heading out onto the main road of the village. She'd have smiled if only she could have seen the roses, their early show of colour, their first proper display. She'd have gently teased him that at last her green fingers were rubbing off on him and who'd have thought he'd have taken so well to rose propagation almost so well as he'd taken to being a village vicar, all those years ago.

The years of wondering what had happened to his wife, Carolina, hadn't even dented his love for her, as heady still as the scent of the rose, but the fear of what may have really kept her away wriggled inside him like a maggot on a newly fallen apple. Everyone had an opinion, from his former parishioners to the police.

'There is no law against leaving,' said the police sergeant who had refused to consider Carolina might be missing. 'Wives leave husbands all the time and the other way round. I'm surprised my wife hasn't left me yet.'

Tea and sympathy flowed from many regulars to his sermons, but others drifted away from the congregation, as if by staying they might catch something; for where there was gossip there was sin, and it may be contagious.

Only Cedric's daughter, Scarlett, all grown up and staunchly independent, ventured words he held onto dearly. 'She must have had her reasons, Dad. Don't blame her until you know them.'

But as the weeks became months and the months became years, no reasons ever came, no words either. A cool breeze made Cedric turn up the collar of his jacket, a jacket Carolina would hate.

'Just because you're a vicar doesn't mean you have to dress like one.' He smiled as he remembered those words. The corduroy jacket, which kept out the evening chill, had been a find in the Oxfam shop in town and it was comfy and frankly suited his mood. He was getting old; he could feel himself ageing with every new day without her and anyway it went well with his dark brown hair and his moustache which he kept well-trimmed. If his hair line receded any further, he'd add a flat cap too, though Scarlett had threatened to disown him if he did.

He approached the village hall which was looking all the better for a fresh coat of paint and a general weed all round. The truth was the garden helped keep him grounded in the new life he tried to navigate without her. As Cedric reached the door, he could already hear voices inside, the scraping of chairs being arranged and Janine's laughter. And just as he did, back when he'd been preparing to enter a service, he had his words already prepared. He entered the village hall as chairman of the historical society. No one saw the man inside, clinging onto routine to keep himself afloat.

'I'd rather hoped we'd have a speaker for the winter gap in our calendar,' said Janine, settling herself down rather too cosily beside Cedric.

'No one wants to turn out in November,' he said, shifting his chair away from her, her perfume so invasive he had to stifle a sneeze.

The Historical Society, its title grander than its reality, met in the village hall on the first Monday of the month. Cedric rather liked the loose nature of its meetings, and the members never ceased to inspire him. His novel, almost two thirds written, was taking shape nicely and with such an intriguing mix of villagers around him he couldn't be blamed for adding a sprinkling of their quirkiness to his cast. Though he couldn't help feeling just a shade guilty at how Janine had morphed into a dreadful antagonist with secrets which would have made the real Janine blush brighter pink than her lambswool cardigan.

But what he felt even more guilty about was his idea, something which had crept into every aspect of his days recently, like ivy crawling over a wall and the more he tried to convince himself he simply didn't have the requisite skills, the more he yearned to prove himself wrong. It was all Janine's fault, her annoying habit of discussing the newspaper headlines as if she'd personally known the people whose lives had been ripped apart. She savoured every detail. At last month's meeting she bored everyone with the story from the national press.

Edging uncomfortably close to Cedric at tea break, she'd shared the news as if tragedy nourished her. 'The poor family,' she said, squeezing the teabag against the side of her cup. 'They thought he'd just got up and left. Stress you know, it gets to people. Nothing unusual about that but then he turns up months later in a wheelie bin at a boarded-up house in a housing estate.' She took a sip of her tea, leaving her scarlet lipstick around the rim. 'Murdered, can you imagine that?'

It made Cedric think, more than he cared to but once he'd started, he couldn't stop. What if people who appeared to have just left were actually missing all along? And then he thought about Carolina, and he hadn't stopped since.

'Well,' said Janine, now slurping the last of her tea. 'What shall we do for our November meeting?'

The other members looked expectantly at Cedric, all except Malcolm. 'I've been researching the families in Ablegate's churchyard,' he offered, preparing to stand up. His fair isle tank top sported a cluster of moth holes in the front and his white peppered hair shed dandruff onto his shoulders.

'Do sit down,' interrupted Janine, the official minute taker and the maker of the teas. 'Are you offering to be our speaker, Malcolm?'

Malcolm's previous talk, on the history of Pembleton's village well, had been presented to just three members, Cedric, and Janine amongst them. Constantine later confessed she'd only attended because she'd thought Malcolm's talk had been due the following month.

'Of course,' continued Malcolm. 'The Watson family have four generations buried in the graveyard of Ablegate church.'

Cedric inwardly groaned. He'd taken a service at Ablegate church a few years back, in fact it was at the end of that very service when the first rumours had circulated about Carolina. She'd not attended, which was unlike her, and the rumours had matured into gossip soon after; a gossip as pernicious as the weeds that wrapped themselves around the gravestones at the furthest point of the graveyard under the shade of the monkey puzzle tree. When later, Cedric had asked his wife why she hadn't attended she just said she'd had a headache and needed a lie down. But surely, she couldn't have had a headache each time she failed to join the congregation or left early before he'd had a chance to bid his worshippers farewell at the door? Yet it had become a thorny issue, one he thought best to avoid, for later she would embrace him so warmly, her touch a magnet to his soul, that he dared do nothing to lose it.

'I was thinking we could open the session up to a more general discussion,' proffered Cedric.

'About what, exactly?' asked Janine, picking up her pen.

Despite Malcolm's lack of originality, Cedric was rather fond of him and anyway, it didn't do to alienate yourself from fellow villagers so, thinking on his feet, Cedric said,

'The valuable use of Ancestry.Com.'

Malcolm's eyes took on a sparkle and Janine, mightily relieved, noted it down.

The rest of the meeting was somewhat subdued, and Cedric was back home by eight thirty, drinking a cup of Earl Grey. When he'd moved in, he'd had no aspirations to re-decorate what was admittedly a rather jaded 1960's bungalow, complete with pebble dash on the outside walls, but Scarlett had other ideas.

'You may be living alone now, but you're not going to live like some kind of shabby hermit,' she'd said. 'You'll make new friends and want to invite them back, so these walls need new paint, and that carpet has stains, and I don't even want to know what they are. Oh, and no magnolia either, you have a personality, and you need to show it.'

In the time that Cedric had lived there, he'd grown accustomed to the new brown leather sofa and the burgundy cushions, he could even tolerate the modern glass coffee table that stood on a beige striped rug and had been a bargain, according to Scarlett. But the one maroon feature wall was a bit much and he'd since toyed with the idea of buying a tin of magnolia paint. But he rather liked the mantelpiece that Scarlett had sanded down herself and stained. Upon it sat a row of framed photographs: Scarlett as a small child, as a teenager and as she was now. He'd wanted to keep a picture of Carolina, she was so photogenic, with her auburn locks and long slender figure, but Scarlett said that would probably look weird. So, Cedric kept one in the drawer of his bedside cabinet instead.

Rubens, his cat, and constant companion these days, rubbed up against Cedric's ankle. Cedric placed a piece of his marmalade cake on the floor for Rubens then finished the last of the slice himself, but it lay heavy on his stomach long after his tea had gone cold. He couldn't stop thinking about Carolina and the story Janine had regaled about the murdered man. For the duration of their marriage, all thirty years of it, she'd been as steady as the tick of the carriage clock on the mantelpiece; as reliable as the chimes on the hour; until that day she took the bus from the village with her small green case, the very same that she'd used on their honeymoon for the weekend in Devon. She'd left no note but had left the breakfast dishes in the sink and her lipstick on the edge of a half-drunk cup of tea. He often wondered what it was he'd said, what thing he hadn't done; what unforgivable sin he'd committed. But he couldn't recall anything being different. He was perhaps foolish enough to have believed in contentment. Though as the years had passed the pain had fractionally eased, the emptiness seemed as encompassing as ever.

The vicar's wife has left him.

He couldn't forget those words. Even taking early retirement and moving out of the parish had done nothing to diminish their hurt. He'd begun the historical society as a means to fill his time, especially in the winter when it was too inclement to labour in the garden. Though it had often occurred to him that it wasn't for him that he was growing it, but for Carolina who was as good with plants as he was with words. Deep down, he didn't believe she'd left him. And now he was sure there was a clue left hidden if only he knew where to look. She couldn't have deserted him, for her touch had been as honest as the words of his God.

It wasn't just that he was sure she loved him, he had a gut feeling that something must have happened to her. Janine's recounting of the tragic story of murder cemented that fear harder still. Carolina had been gone two days when the telephone had rung, it was a Thursday evening. He knew the time because the six o'clock news had just started on the television, and he'd been eating his supper off a tray on his lap. When he answered, first there was nothing but then he heard what sounded like something clattering to the ground, followed by a small gasp and then the line had gone dead. He was sure it had been Carolina, and he was still sure now and it unnerved him dreadfully. The police had been less than unhelpful.

'If it were your wife calling, Sir,' the police sergeant had said, 'maybe she just changed her mind. There's no law against that.'

No, Carolina was missing. He scooped up Rubens and stroked the cat's smooth ginger fur. He wondered how many people went missing every day and once he started to research it, he was staggered by the number of people who seemed to just simply vanish. His obsession grew, reaching out tendrils that flourished. It had grown out of his pain, nurtured by the crime thrillers he read every night because sleep refused to visit. Now, sitting with Rubens purring on his lap, his very soul was telling him, Carolina hadn't come home because she couldn't.

Printed in Great Britain
by Amazon

62709588R00143